Also by Michael Bonfrisco
Smart Estate Planning in New Jersey

Also by Dennis D. Duffy
Legacy Planning: A Guide to Preserving Your Family Wealth (2012)
Estate Planning Basics: A Crash Course in Safeguarding Your Legacy (2008)

The Modern Investor

The Modern Investor

WHY MOST INVESTORS FAIL AND WHAT YOU CAN DO ABOUT IT

Michael Bonfrisco

Foreword by:
Dennis D. Duffy
Ryan M. Denman

ISBN-13: 9781517789879
ISBN-10: 1517789877

Contents

Foreword ·xi

Introduction
Why Most Investors Fail and What You Can Do About It · · · · · · · · · · xv

Part 1
Understanding Investments:
Building Your Foundation

Question 1:
Do You Have an Investment Philosophy? · 3

Question 2:
What Are The Critical Ingredients To Being A Successful Investor? · · · 11

Question 3:
What Is An Asset Class, And Why Is It Important
For My Portfolio? · 15

Question 4:
I Own a Bunch of Different Stuff in My Portfolio,
so I'm Diversified, Right? · 19

Question 5:

Why Do I Need to Rebalance My Portfolio Periodically? · · · · · · · · · · 25

Question 6:

When It Comes to My Advisor, What's the Difference
Between a Facilitator and a Fiduciary? · 29

Part 2

**The Science of Evidence Based, Structured
Investing: How It All Works**

Question 7:

How Is Wealth Created, and Why Is This
Important to Understand? · 35

Question 8:

How Do I Know if My Portfolio Is Delivering the Best
Expected Return for the Amount of Risk I Am Taking On? · · · · · · · · · 41

Question 9:

In Today's World Where Information Travels
at Lightning Speed, How Can Any Investor Gain an Edge? · · · · · · · · · 49

Question 10:

Why Does It Seem Like the Market Is
Completely Random? · 53

Question 11:

Aren't Some Companies Poised to Be Better than
Others, and How Do I Figure that Out ahead of Time? · · · · · · · · · · · 57

Part 3
Speculating and Gambling with Your Money:
What We Know Does Not Work

Question 12:
I Like to Pick My Own Companies; Why Doesn't
Stock Picking Work? · 63

Question 13:
I Like to Get In and Out of the
Market to Avoid Downturns;
Why Doesn't Market Timing Work? · 67

Question 14:
I Like to Invest Only in the Areas of the Market that
Seem to Be on the Rise. Why Shouldn't I Chase Hot Sectors? · · · · · · · 71

Question 15:
What Are the Costs in Investing?
Are There Hidden Costs in My Portfolio? · 75

Question 16:
Why Isn't Gold a Good Investment Choice? · · · · · · · · · · · · · · · · · · · 81

Question 17:
Why Aren't Indexed Annuities a Good Option for My Portfolio? · · · · · 85

Part 4
The Battle of Logic and Knowledge
Over Fear and Emotion

Question 18:
I Know the Market Is Due for a Correction.
Don't I Need to Protect My Nest Egg? · 91

Question 19:
I Am Afraid of Losing All of My Money,
Why Do I Need To Invest in the Market at All? · · · · · · · · · · · · · · · · · 95

Question 20:
How Does the Media Derail My Investment Peace of Mind? · · · · · · · · 99

Question 21:
How Does Asset Class Based Structured Investing
Compare to Passive Indexed Investing and Active Trading? · · · · · · · · 103

Question 22:
Now that I Know How a Prudent Portfolio
Is Created, Why Can't I Do This All on My Own? · · · · · · · · · · · · · · 107

EndNotes · 111

Foreword

When I became an estate planning attorney more than 25 years ago, I routinely dealt with families, their assets and money. Over the years, I saw far too many clients get blindsided by the traditional delivery of financial services. Hidden conflicts of interest were everywhere, and even though I had a finance undergraduate degree, an M.B.A. and a business background, I learned that I too had fallen victim to the same myths that hurt most investors. Eventually, I learned that "*I did not know what I did not know.*" I realized, these traps were causing me and my client's continuous pain, frustration, anxiety and worry.

I discovered that financial planning and the development of a financial plan are very often used as a sales or marketing tool to sell a firm's financial products. And of course, the sale of these financial products produces a commission on the plan's recommendations. Unfortunately, the investor rarely knows whether or not the plan's recommendations are in their best interest or in the best interest of the planner and his/her firm. In addition, the majorities of planners work for a brokerage firm or insurance company. They do not really work directly for the client. As a result, the brokerage firm or insurance company actually controls what products the planner can recommend to clients.

Next, the traditional planning model does very little to educate investors and help them deal with the instincts and emotions that are at the root of a poor investment experience. Almost no effort is given to help clients learn how markets work and how to achieve true peace of mind when investing. If the plan involves choosing the best manager and trying to beat the market, it will invariably fail.

Finding how to help my clients learn to make sure they were dealing with a fiduciary who acts in a client's best interest *at all times* became a virtually obsession for me. When Ryan joined my law firm in 2011, his background in economics allowed him to learn and apply these lessons for all our clients at the beginning of his career, with expertise well beyond his years.

As a result of these traps, our client's need for estate planning was greatly impacted by their failure to succeed in their financial and investment lives. Some were hurt so badly they withdrew from the markets and decided they would concede they would never achieve their retirement or legacy goals.

Once we learned the truth, we became passionate about ensuring the families we work with were given many opportunities to get the financial education they need and learn the academic evidence to achieve financial success. Coaching clients to ask the right questions and to know what they did not know became our calling and part of our daily life. Rest assured, you have in your hand the answer to these problems and a solution to be a more successful investor and achieve a happier life.

We are optimists. We believe in the abundance of the free market enterprise system. History and evidence tell us that an economic system centered on individuals having free choice will prosper over other systems. Our free enterprise system, although not perfect, has created more comfort and wealth than any other approach that has been tried. We believe in our ability to create wealth and prosperity out of hard work and ingenuity and that the best way to capture this wealth in our investments is with the prudent application of ownership in the companies that create wealth. No one can predict the future, so we believe in the science of diversification in efficient markets around the world.

We believe successful investing requires the advice and coaching of professionals who are trained in the art and science of human behavior, because fear and other emotions often drive even the most level headed investor to make the wrong choices.

We hope this book provides you with guidance and direction to succeed at your life dreams – the lessons contained in it did that for us!

Dennis D. Duffy & Ryan M. Denman
Estate Planning Attorneys & Wealth Coaches

INTRODUCTION

Why Most Investors Fail and What You Can Do About It

This book was written to help shed light on a confusing and often misunderstood topic. Most investors have little understanding of what is actually happening in the market or in their investment portfolio. After speaking to countless investors over the years, I have learned that many of them have a vague concept of how the securities markets actually work and where returns come from. It's been my experience that too many people feel it's necessary to find the next hot stock or chase a sector of the market. They ask, "Got any stock tips?" Others feel it's important to look for the best money manager or investment guru and think that by searching for a person who has experience in stock picking, they will end up with a better return. Other investors think it's a matter of timing the market by looking for the right time to jump in and out in order to participate in positive returns while avoiding downturns. Unfortunately, all three of these techniques simply do not work. The most worrying problem I see is that so many investors entrust their entire life savings to people and an industry that they don't really understand.

My own history with investing follows a similar path of misinformation and folly. I fell for every single trap that I advise against now. I chased the hot sector of technology companies right into the ground. I looked at last year's five-star mutual funds to tell me which funds would be good next year. I jumped in and out of the market, constantly trying to catch the up swells. After about a decade of lackluster results, it began to dawn on me that either I wasn't as bright as I had told myself I was, or something else was going on in the market.

All of this started me on a journey that forever changed my life. A good friend pointed me toward a few books that would help shed light on just what mistakes I was making with my investments. The first was a huge best seller on index investing written by Burton Malkiel, *A Random Walk Down Wall Street*. The second was called *Winning at the Loser's Game*, by Charles Ellis. I felt these books must have been written with investors like me in mind because they nailed my problem right from the start. I began to have a deeper understanding of what was going on in my portfolio, and more importantly, I changed my thinking about the investing industry.

The essential view put forth in my research was simple yet profound. No one—not me, not Warren Buffet, not Jim Cramer, and not the people who work on Wall Street—can predict the future, and thus no one can predict the market. To think otherwise is to claim an ability that is simply not bestowed on mere mortals. This simple premise lay at the heart of an approach to investing that has stayed with me ever since. The facts were in, and academics had pieced together a tapestry to create a better picture of how the markets really work and backed up their claims with actual evidence.

One of the core tenants of the academic approach to investing is that the market disseminates information efficiently and quickly. Only new and unknowable information changes the price of an investment, and therefore, no one can consistently predict where the market is headed before others. The concept that the markets are efficient was first put forth by Noble-Prize-winning economist Eugene Fama. He and others like him, many from the University of Chicago Booth School of Economics, have been beating the drum for decades that *passively structured* investment portfolios will outperform the vast majority of their *actively* traded counterparts, especially when costs are deducted.

The genesis for this new way of looking at the market began in earnest in the late 1960s into the 1970s. The concept of index fund investing took shape as a direct result of these principles. John Bogle, who studied at Princeton University, launched the first publicly available S&P 500 index fund in 1975 with his then start-up mutual fund company, The Vanguard Group. Now, most retail mutual fund families offer at least some index funds. Bogle led the charge for the low-cost passive index fund, and investors responded.

In the early 1990s, Fama and his longtime collaborator, Kenneth French, went further than simple index funds. They wanted to show how certain asset classes had a higher expected return for their associated risk. They developed a widely understood economic model called the Three-Factor Model. The model explained how one could harness the best returns that the market could offer, assuming a certain level of volatility. While basic index funds were better than actively traded funds, Fama and French showed where the best expected returns came from and how to access them.

In the past thirty years, the investment firm Dimensional Fund Advisors (DFA) has pioneered the application of their academic principles. DFA and their collaborators, like Matson Money and others, assembled various asset classes in the right proportions to create prudent portfolios that seek to capture market returns in the most efficient and risk-adjusted manner. As of the end of the first quarter of 2015, DFA reported over $398 billion invested in their funds, making them a quiet giant in the industry.

Too few main street investors know about any of this groundbreaking work or how to access it. They assume that all fund companies and investment firms offer the same basic services. Even with the popularity of some indexing funds and DFA, most funds are actively managed. This means that the money managers are seeking to capture exceptional returns without associated risks. They claim that they can do this because of their superior skills and abilities. They think their experience and data are just that much better than the next firm's and boast that overall, they will outperform the pack. In doing so, they try to pick the winners and sell the losers before others understand the true value of an investment. They promise to tactically sell off investments before the market turns down and pick up shares at the bottom of the market, right before an upswing.

In the decades that active managers have been trying to beat the market, we should assume that some would have consistent verifiable evidence to support their claims. But the evidence on managers' ability to outsmart the market is clear—they can't do it. According to David Swenson of the Yale University Endowment Fund, 96 percent of active funds failed to beat a simple S&P 500 index fund. Of the few that are fortunate enough to come out ahead, their ability to do so consistently appears to be random. There is little or no correlation between a manager's ability to pick stocks in the past successfully with his or her ability to do so in the future. Even if there was a time many years ago when managers could take advantage of mispricing in the market, that time is long past. Technology has completely changed the investing landscape. Gone are the days when Warren Buffet could pore over financial reports and find, as he said it, "old cigar butts on the street that had a few good puffs left in them."

No market is perfectly efficient, but the securities market is as close as we can get. Today, as we all know, information spreads worldwide at lightning speed. Top-notch universities mint thousands of new MBAs, mathematicians, statisticians, and economists every year who are ready to take over the world. Millions of people have access to the same information simultaneously. Countless traders, both professional and novice, are glued to computer monitors, poring over data to look for pricing discrepancies and mistakes. Where such opportunities may exist, they are almost instantly closed. Thousands of computers continuously scan prices against multiple criteria to detect mispricing. Hundreds of analysts follow a single stock. There are few, if any, secrets. If there are a few nuggets, the main street investor can't compete with the rest of the market in order to find them for his or her portfolio.

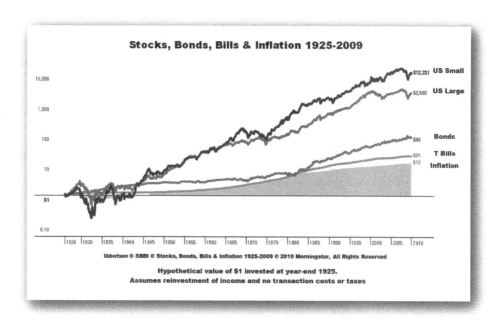

If the past century of our collective history is any indication, the long-term trend for the equities is decidedly clear: they are headed up. On average, in three out of four years, the stock market is positive. The problem, of course, is that there is no way to predict which years it's going to be positive and which years it's not. According to Ibbotson Research, since 1926, US large companies have returned an annualized compound rate of about 9.9 percent. Other asset classes, like US small companies, have fared even better, delivering about 12 percent returns over time.

No other investment can compete with equities, quite simply because stocks best harness the great engine of wealth creation. Through a turbulent century, with the 1930s' global depression, two World Wars, the Cold War and many other conflicts, dozens of recessions, and countless natural disasters, businesses in a free enterprise system have still found a way to prosper. Firms of all sizes have created value to the consumer and generated profits for shareholders and wages for employees. Equity in those companies, in the form of owning shares of its stock, is the translation of that wealth. It is clear that equities are the greatest wealth creation tool that this planet has ever known. As investors, our ability to harness this natural phenomenon in a prudent, efficient way is the key to creating real wealth for our families.

This book seeks to set out the case for structured investing, which is designing a passively engineered securities portfolio of varying asset classes in precise proportions, in order to capture the best expected return for a given level of risk. In doing this, we are going to dive deep into the concepts of active versus structured investing. We are going to understand the cost of capital and that there is no such thing as a free lunch. Further, we will explore the pervasive superstitions that Wall Street wants you to believe and how to move past them and become a modern investor.

I have assembled this book in a question-and-answer format. There are twenty-two essential questions that are set out in the succeeding chapters. The answers to the questions will build your understanding of how the market actually works, where returns come from, and why stock picking, market timing, and track record investing do not work consistently or predictably. While you will not learn everything there is to know about investing, what you will be left with is enough good quality information so that you can make intelligent, logical investment decisions that will guide you for a lifetime.

PART 1

UNDERSTANDING INVESTMENTS: BUILDING YOUR FOUNDATION

QUESTION 1

Do You Have an Investment Philosophy?

What is your investment philosophy? This is a question that few investors have ever actually considered, though it is the first and most important question you should answer before you make an investment.
You need to decide on your personal investment philosophy, because the
side that you fall on will dictate how you choose the particular investments
in your portfolio. It's not enough to say that your investment philosophy is
anything that makes a good return or that you want only the investments
that have little or no risk. That is not a philosophy, but rather a goal or a
wish. While many people have goals for where they want their portfolio to
go, they don't realize that having a strong investment philosophy is what
puts an investor on the right path toward obtaining these goals. Without
this clear plan in place, an investor is like a rudderless sailboat, drifting all
over the sea in the direction of the changing winds. Having an investment
philosophy allows investors to have a greater appreciation of what is happening with their investments and greater peace of mind that their investment goals are being accomplished.

There are two fundamental views of the stock market: the traditional
active approach and the efficient market approach. The most common
style of investing is the traditional active approach. The vast majority of
investors employ this strategy (either directly or through their money

managers). People with a traditional view believe that individual investors with enough good, quality information can predict where the market is headed and thereby outsmart the rest of us. They believe that the market is inefficient or that markets do not work. The basis of this theory is that when it comes to the price of stock, the market often has it wrong. All of the information available to all of the millions of investors is somehow not currently reflected in the price of stocks. By finding the stocks that are priced incorrectly, active investors believe they can get superior returns and reduce or eliminate their investment risk in the process.

Believers in this concept are all around us. They are constantly comparing and contrasting in hopes of finding hidden deals that they believe the rest of us do not see. They might be the golf buddy who is exuberant about the next great company that's ready to explode or the uncle who watches business news programs all day and night. In believing that the stock market is something one can predict, traditional investors need to have new and fresh information constantly to make decisions. They are always plugged into the news to keep up with the constant stream of data from the changing market, in order to make adjustments to their portfolios accordingly. These investors often point out anecdotal examples of when they bought some stock before it took off because they just knew that it was a great company. Each time active investors make a prediction correctly, it reinforces their belief that they have a real ability to outmaneuver the market. Instead of being discouraged when their predications fail to come to fruition, many active investors instead feel that they would be more successful if only they had more information available. This further perpetuates the active investing cycle.

To be clear, most investors—both professionals and amateurs—subscribe to the traditional, inefficient market concept, even though the overwhelming evidence is that it provides no added returns to their portfolio. There is simply no verification that this method has consistently and predictably outperformed the market as a whole. Research has actually proved that the reverse is true—the costs of active trading subtract returns from many portfolios. It is estimated that the cost of active trading puts an additional 3.35 percent drag on performance. This means that an active trader would need his or her portfolio to produce another 3.35 percent of returns annually, just to keep pace with the market.[1]

Compounding the problem further with the active approach is the increased buying and selling that goes on in active portfolios. It is estimated that institutional investors are involved in 90 percent of all trades.[1] This means that when an average investor puts in a trade to buy or sell a stock, he or she is most likely trading with a huge institutional trader. Institutional investors are organizations like banks, retirement or pension funds, hedge funds, and mutual funds. The people who run these organizations are top professionals in the financial industry and have access to all of the best information. Common sense tells us that the average investor is not as likely to be on the winning side of this equation. The professional has the advantage of knowledge and experience. It would be like an average person playing basketball one-on-one against Michael Jordan. There is no possibility that the average person can win. The problem for main street investors is that they have no idea whom they are playing against. In a stock trade, there is always a winner and a loser, and if the average Joe knew that he was playing against an MVP, he might not be so sure about his decision.

Here is a thought: what if the only reason investors followed the traditional market approach was because they never actually considered that there was an alternative? What if, when presented with all of the facts, evidence, and a fresh set of eyes, investors could make an informed decision about which investment philosophy fits their sensibilities?

There are ways to invest without using active trading. The most well-known uses the *efficient market hypothesis*, which is often called the "efficient market approach." The efficient market hypothesis ("EMH") was popularized by Professor Eugene Fama of the University of Chicago Booth School of Economics. The main principle of EMH is the belief that the market works. EMH essentially states that at any given time and in a liquid market, security prices fully reflect all available information. This means that the best determinant of the price of a stock is usually based on the demand for that stock. In addition, all known information about the stock is already factored into the current price.

EMH says that a company's stock prices will go up or down because the market swiftly responds to current conditions and efficiently incorporates that data into the price of stocks. This is based on observable proof that shows that the market responds to new information incredibly quickly. For example, if a company announced that earnings were better than expected, then the demand for that company's stock may increase and the price per share moves up. If investors were not willing to pay more for a company that announced better-than-expected earnings, the stock price for that company would not have gone up. The news of the increased earnings was quickly absorbed by investors and incorporated into the price of the stock by the market. This means that every time an investor purchases a stock, the price he or she paid is the best estimate of the intrinsic value of that company.

EMH also focuses on the idea that because no one can predict the future, trying to do so is foolish and will hurt your portfolio returns. Rather than try to guess which stocks might perform well, those who accept EMH hold portfolios with a very broad basket of stocks and bonds. This is called diversification, and gives the investor the best expected level of return for a given level of risk.

Efficient Market Approach	Traditional Approach
The Market Works	The Market Does Not Work
Own Equities (With Fixed Income)	Stock Picking
Diversify Globally	Market Timing
Rebalance Periodically	Track Record Investing

Understanding these two different fundamental approaches is at the core of moving forward with a game plan that can lead to long-term success. When I consult with investors and lay out the two competing investment philosophies, most people indicate that they believe in the efficient market approach. They almost always say something like, "No one can predict the future, and only a fool would try to do so." Yet when I ask some questions about how they actually invest, I see that their actions really match up with the traditional inefficient approach. There is a disconnect between what they say they believe and what they actually do.

So now it's your opportunity to rethink everything you ever thought you knew about how the market works and see it in a whole new way, as a beginner, without preconceived notions. Would you be interested to see what the result would be? Most people, when asked this question, will say, "Sure, I am interested in learning new things." I can tell you from experience that it's not that simple. First, you need to accept that there is a chance that your old way of looking at investing could be wrong and everything your instincts are telling you may not make any sense when it comes to the market. You should also accept that substantial evidence, research, and academic study may lead you toward a different conclusion.

Around the year 1850, germ theory was not accepted by the medical community. Doctors and scientists did not believe that most diseases, like cholera and the plague, were caused by microscopic bugs we call germs. The popular theory then was that disease was caused by bad smells, especially in the night air. This was called the miasma theory. This theory was first popularized in the Middle Ages and was accepted as truth for hundreds of years. People in this time period really believed that if a fog came in with a stench, you were doomed.

Doctors prescribed that people carry around flowers in their pockets and sniff them to ward off disease. Worse yet, they specifically rejected the germ theory and ridiculed its proponents because of the widespread belief that disease came from foul odors. The government took no measures to keep sewage away from drinking water. The thought of raw sewage mixed with our drinking water today is unfathomable. But if you had no clue as to the origins of disease and the science behind what was actually going on, then the foul odor theory would be plausible. If you were taught this theory as a young person, you would accept it as fact without questioning it later in life.

The germ theory was not accepted as fact until the science was developed to prove it to be true. Suddenly, measures could be taken to prevent germs from spreading. As time went on and more and more information about germs was discovered, miasma theory began to seem unfounded. How could smelling a bag of potpourri ever protect someone from a communicable disease?

You might be saying to yourself, "This is interesting, but what does it have to do with my investment portfolio?" The history of the efficient market theory is remarkably similar. Efficient market theory is actually not a new concept. Eugene Fama first wrote about it in the late 1960s in his doctoral thesis. However, it wasn't until decades later that the science was available to show that Dr. Fama was correct. As recently as 2013, he was awarded the Nobel Prize in economics for the work that he had done in the 1960s. The academic community has become very familiar with the concept, earning Dr. Fama the unofficial title of a "father of modern finance." The evidence points away from the ability to predict what the market will do in the short term, the same way evidence once pointed away from bad smells as a cause of disease.

Unfortunately, Wall Street and the media largely ignore the fact that the traditional approach is flatly unsupported by the empirical evidence, mostly because it does not serve their best interests. After all, the efficient market theory speaks to the fact that no one can predict where the market will go in the short term. As a result, active trading is discouraged. What will the business news shows speak to if not the latest trends and forecasts? If there are no predictions for the future, these shows will go off the air. Wall Street earns fees, commissions, and profits from the activity of trading, regardless of the winners and the losers. A concept that recommends that active trading is a waste would not support their business plan of promoting active and frequent trading.

Recently, investors have begun to catch on to the efficient market concepts and embrace them. I believe that in time, the traditional active market approach will become outdated. Trying to pick winners and losers, use market timing, and look to the past as a way to predict the future will be rejected and discarded, just as the miasma theory of bad smells was discarded over 150 years ago. For investors, deciding which theory they accept as true and correlating their investments to their beliefs is vital for long-term happiness and success.

The Short Answer:

- **Investors need a philosophy in order to ensure that their investments match up with their long-term goals.**

QUESTION 2

What Are The Critical Ingredients To Being A Successful Investor?

S uccessful investing is not only capturing expected returns from reliable methods but also managing avoidable risk. These risks include holding too few securities; betting on countries or sectors of the economy; following market predictions; speculating on currency movements, oil demands, or interest rate fluctuations; and relying on information from financial gurus, who, despite their claims, are wrong more than they are right. Being a successful investor and curbing these risks really comes down to four essential components: owning equities with fixed income, being globally diversified, rebalancing your portfolio periodically, and staying disciplined with the help of an advisor or coach.

The first component of successful investing is that a portfolio must include equities. Equities are the stock portion of your portfolio. When you own equities, or stock, you are securing an ownership position in a company. By owning companies, you drive up the returns in your portfolio. The reason for this is that companies create the goods and services that keep our economy thriving. A company's profits are then returned to investors in the share price of the stock, or its dividends, increasing the value of your portfolio.

Your portfolio needs a way to balance the ups and downs of stocks. Using fixed-income investments, like treasuries and bonds, can make a portfolio less volatile. Being diversified with equities and fixed income is the second component of successful investing. Nobel laureates Harry Markowitz, William Sharpe, and Merton Miller pioneered our understanding of how diversification works in a portfolio. Markowitz showed that by owning varying asset classes, like equities and bonds, which have dissimilar price movements, investors could increase their expected returns and decrease their risk. Fixed income investments are typically less risky, and they counteract the movement of equities. Often, when bonds are down, equities are up and vice versa. Since these asset classes move in different directions, this smoothes out the ups and downs of a portfolio. Many investment portfolios I have seen have both intermediate bonds and US large stocks, but this is where it often stops. To have true diversification, you would want to have more than just two asset classes in your portfolio, which I explore further in Question 4. A truly diversified portfolio may have about twenty separate and distinct asset classes, holding thousands of unique securities all over the world.

The third component of the formula is to rebalance your portfolio periodically. That is, you have to sell the high part of the portfolio and buy low investments. We have all heard the expression, "buy low and sell high." That is how your portfolio should work as well, buying when prices are low and selling when the value is higher. Let's say that your US large asset class is doing great this year; it's up 15 percent. Your international small cap, on the other hand, is not so great, and is down 5 percent. To keep your portfolio balanced, at the end of the period, your portfolio manager will sell off some of your high-priced US large and buy up some of the discounted international.

The final element to be a successful investor is to stay consistent and disciplined with the assistance of a coach or advisor. One of the biggest mistakes that investors make is that they fail to stay consistent with their plan. We all know the secret to losing weight. It comes down to doing more of two critical things. We need to consistently move our bodies more, and we need to consume fewer calories. The hundreds, if not thousands, of books on the subject have these two core attributes in common. Every year, millions of Americans (myself included) vow to get in shape and eat right as a New Year's resolution. Yet, within a few weeks or so, they often drift. Without a trainer or weight-loss coach to keep them on track, they often stop eating right or exercising consistently. Successful investing is no different, and investors fall into the same traps. They will pick up a magazine or book on investing and spend the time to get organized. Then the first time there is a market hiccup or news of a hot new investment option, they break the basic investing rules.

We all like to believe that we can stay consistent long term. After all, the rules for successful investing are straightforward. Moving from one investment scheme to another often results in disaster to your returns. Chasing the hot stock or looking to the past to try to predict the future will decrease your expected return and will likely increase your volatility. In the end, without a trained advisor to help provide discipline, few investors achieve satisfactory results. An advisor or coach reminds the investors of the rules and keeps them on the right track to have a successful portfolio.

The Short Answer:

- **To be successful, investors should always own equities in proportion to fixed income investments suitable to their risk tolerance, be diversified globally, rebalance their portfolio periodically, and stay disciplined for the long term with an investment coach.**

QUESTION 3

What Is An Asset Class, And Why Is It Important For My Portfolio?

An asset class is a group of securities that have similar financial characteristics and behave in the same way in the marketplace. Broadly, the three main asset classes are equities (stocks), fixed-income (treasuries and bonds), and cash equivalents (money market instruments). Most investment portfolios focus on equities and fixed income, so it is important to have a good understanding of how these two asset classes work.

Equities are often classified by market capitalization. Market capitalization is just a name for a pretty basic concept: it is the market value of a company's outstanding shares. This figure is found by taking the stock price and multiplying it by the total number of shares outstanding. This means that in the market, companies are grouped together in accordance with the size of the company and not the price of the stock. Based on these figures, stocks are commonly broken down into large-, medium-, small-, and micro cap groupings. These distinctions are important to make, as every category will perform differently in the market. Since each category differs in performance, an investor should own these groups in special proportions in order to capture the best returns and offset volatility.

Companies are also categorized in another way—value or growth—based on the health and earnings of the company. Again, the distinction is important because they behave differently. Growth companies are essentially healthy, robust companies with good long-term prospects. They are usually financially fit, often with a history of paying additional income to investors in the form of dividends. Growth companies are not just exciting technology companies like Apple Inc. and Google, but also boring companies like General Electric and Caterpillar. Large growth stocks are often referred to as blue chip stocks.

Value companies are the opposite of growth companies. These are firms that don't have the established history and strength that growth companies do. A value company might be an older company that has fallen on rough times or a new firm struggling to establish itself in the market. For this reason, they are not as healthy; and because these companies are less robust than others, they are riskier investments. That risk translates into a lower relative price than that of growth companies. The intelligent market has adjusted their price to reflect the risk. Value companies also have an enormous potential for expansion, meaning they could have a greater possible future return.

Fixed income investments are also essential to have in an investment portfolio. They are more commonly known as treasuries or bonds and are generally sorted by duration. Short-term fixed income will behave differently in the market than long-term bonds. Typically, short- and intermediate-term fixed income securities with one- to five-year durations are added to a portfolio to diversify and to reduce volatility.

However, not all bonds are used to offset stock market volatility. One of the important distinctions with long-term bonds is that they are very sensitive to interest rate fluctuations. When rates rise, bond prices fall and vice versa. Bond price movements are predominantly determined by what's called duration, which is a measure of their interest rate sensitivity. For instance, a thirty-year bond with duration of twenty will move approximately 20 percent for a one-point change in rates. The reason for this is because bonds are actually fixed-rate loans. When you purchase a bond, the company agrees to pay you a certain interest rate for that fixed amount of time. In the future, if a person can borrow from the government or others for a better rate, then your bonds become less attractive. Long-term bonds often go out for decades, so the impact of the rate change is more profound; small changes in the interest rate have a huge impact on their value. Investors often comment that bonds are safer or less volatile than stocks. This statement is true when referring to short and intermediate fixed income, but it does not apply to long-term bonds.

It's important to understand asset classes when building a portfolio. A well-balanced portfolio should include many different asset classes in precise proportions in order to maximize returns. Putting together an effective portfolio is a lot like baking a cake. To successfully bake a cake, you need to have many different types of ingredients in very specific amounts. It's not enough to have most of the ingredients or all of the ingredients in the wrong amounts. If you want to enjoy your cake, every ingredient needs to be present in exactly the right amount. Your investment portfolio works the same way.

Unfortunately, most investors have only a few asset classes and are not usually aware of the missing pieces in their investments. I commonly see portfolios made up of large growth stocks with some short- and medium-term bonds. There are dozens of different asset classes available, and most investors are missing out on most of them, especially small and value companies, which have exhibited the best long-term returns. The effect of these missing pieces is serious. It means that the main street investor is taking on too much risk for their expected return.

The Short Answer:

- **Asset allocation is the most important aspect when building a successful portfolio, and owning a mix of certain asset classes in the right proportions is vital.**

QUESTION 4

I Own a Bunch of Different Stuff in My Portfolio, so I'm Diversified, Right?

D iversifying your portfolio is one of the most important ways to reach your long-term investing goals while also controlling risk. Diversification enables investors to capture broad market forces while reducing the uncompensated risk associated with individual stocks. When I ask investors if their portfolios are diversified, I often hear a similar reply, "Sure, I'm diversified. I have some stocks and bonds." If I press a little further and ask them what it means to be diversified, I usually get a response along the lines of "Diversification is owning a bunch of different stuff." Diversification, however, does not mean just owning a "bunch of different stuff." You learned about asset classes in Question 3; diversification builds on this. Diversification is achieved through owning a diverse group of asset classes that move in dissimilar directions.

At any given time, certain asset classes are going to move in one direction, while others may move in another direction. For example, domestic small stocks may move in a different direction than international stocks, which move in a different direction than intermediate bonds. While one class is up in the market, another is down. The following graph illustrates how diversification helps to smooth out the ups and downs in your portfolio. Since no two asset classes will ever move perfectly in unison with one another, to create this straight upward line, the principle illustrated here simplifies the concept enough so that we can visualize it.

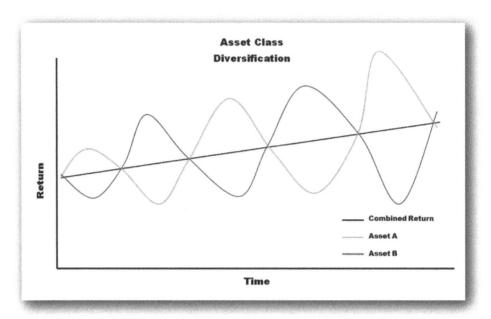

Keep in mind; owning different asset classes is not the same as owning different companies. For instance, let's say I own stock in fifty different large, US companies, such as GE, Apple, Exxon, and so on. Even though I own fifty different stocks, I am not really diversified because most US large stocks move together. At any given time, the direction one stock moves is how they all tend to move. The outside factors that affect one company will affect the others as well. Similarly, owning the thirty companies in the Dow Jones Industrial Average or even all five hundred companies in the S&P 500 is not true diversification either, given that these domestic large-growth companies are all in the same asset class. Therefore, their price fluctuations are correlated. They all tend to respond similarly to market conditions.

There is no asset class that is the best all of the time. The media, financial gurus, and many investors use the S&P 500 or Dow Jones as a corollary for the US market as a whole. Currently, there are about five thousand companies traded on US exchanges. Some of the companies are large, of course, but many are smaller. Many are growth, while others are value. By using the S&P 500, or the biggest five hundred growth companies, as a shortcut to try to describe the returns of all of the others misleads investors and the public as a whole. If the S&P 500 were always the leader, investing would be very simple—you would just buy S&P 500—except no one knows ahead of time which will be the best investment going into the future. We must also remember that large companies are relatively safer than many other stocks and their expected return is less. Since the media only speaks in terms of large companies, like the S&P 500, it's hard, if not impossible, to resist the urge to compare it to your truly diverse portfolio. In those years when the S&P 500 looks great, the inclination is to want to chase that hot sector. Nevertheless, each and every asset class has the possibility of being the best in any one year, as shown in the following chart, compiled from data generally available. An investor in only US large would not have the best possible returns each year.

While investors would prefer to invest only in the assets that are moving up all the time, we all know that this is not actually realistic. The problem with diversification is that sometimes it appears to be pulling down your portfolio returns, when in fact, it is doing everything it was intended to do. This is particularly true when we think that the S&P 500 is doing better than other asset classes.

Let me give you an example of how this plays out in real life. A prudent investor spreads his investments out over most of the US market. He is capturing all the dimensions of return with small and large companies and value and growth stocks. Now, let's say at the end of the year, looking at his statement, he sees that his diverse portfolio has gains of 5 percent. At first, he is not too concerned about this because he knows that some years are going to be better than others. Taking a closer look, he realizes that the US large companies in his portfolio happened to be up 15 percent in that same year. Having a diverse portfolio means that you are not only going to have the investments that are up; you are also going to have the investments that

The Value of Diversification and Asset Classes with Low Correlation Based on the Best and Worst Performing Asset

BEST ← → **WORST**

Year									
2000	US Small Value	Long Term Bonds	US Large Value	Short Term Fixed Income	Cash	US Large Company	International Small	US Small Company	International Large
2001	US Small Company	US Small Value	Short Term Fixed Income	Cash	Long Term Bonds	US Large Value	US Large Company	International Small	International Large
2002	Long Term Bonds	Short Term Fixed Income	Cash	International Small	US Small Value	US Small Company	International Large	US Large Company	US Large Value
2003	US Small Company	US Small Value	International Small	International Large	US Large Company	US Large Value	Short Term Fixed Income	Long Term Bonds	Cash
2004	International Small	US Small Value	International Large	US Large Value	Long Term Bonds	US Large Company	Long Term Bonds	Cash	Short Term Fixed Income
2005	International Small	International Large	US Large Value	US Small Value	US Small Company	US Large Company	US Small Company	Cash	Short Term Fixed Income
2006	International Large	International Small	US Large Value	US Small Value	US Small Company	US Large Company	Cash	Short Term Fixed Income	Long Term Bonds
2007	International Large	Long Term Bonds	International Small	Short Term Fixed Income	US Large Company	Cash	US Large Value	US Small Company	US Small Value
2008	Long Term Bonds	Short Term Fixed Income	Cash	US Small Value	US Large Company	US Large Value	US Small Company	International Large	International Small
2009	US Small Company	International Small	US Small Value	International Large	US Large Company	US Large Value	Short Term Fixed Income	Cash	Long Term Bonds
2010	US Small Company	US Small Value	International Small	US Large Company	US Large Value	Long Term Bonds	International Large	Short Term Fixed Income	Cash
2011	Long Term Bonds	US Large Company	Short Term Fixed Income	Cash	US Large Value	US Small Value	US Small Company	International Large	International Small
2012	US Large Value	US Small Value	International Large	International Small	US Small Company	US Large Company	Long Term Bonds	Short Term Fixed Income	Cash
2013	US Small Company	US Small Value	US Large Value	US Large Company	International Small	International Large	Short Term Fixed Income	Cash	Long Term Bonds
2014	Long Term Bonds	US Large Company	US Large Value	US Small Company	US Small Value	Short Term Fixed Income	Cash	International Large	International Small

go down or are flat. The investor looking at his statement and comparing it to the S&P 500 feels that he lost 10 percent. He thinks if he had just put all his money in the US large this year, he would be way up. But this is a trap. It's called chasing hot sectors, which I discuss in Question 14. No one knows where the market is headed in the future. It's easy to look back now and say that you knew the US large was poised for a great year. But you didn't really know it ahead of time; you just guessed. The evidence shows that investors who chase hot sectors underperform the diversified investor over time.

In the end, the only sound approach is to ignore the media hype and your own hunches about the market in order to recognize that a properly engineered, diverse portfolio will behave differently than one that has all of your investments in just one asset class. Those who keep the long-term horizon in mind and keep themselves educated about how the market works, end up capturing the best that the market can deliver without the need to speculate and gamble. As the following graph illustrates, true diversification would typically occur with the combination of about fifteen to twenty separate asset classes covering more than ten thousand separate and distinct securities in dozens of countries around the world. The selection of these asset classes and the precise proportion of each are essential to a well-designed portfolio.

Simplified Sample Asset Class Mix
65% Equities, 35% Fixed Income

Asset Class	Percent
US Large	9%
US Large Value	9%
US Small	8%
US Small Value	9%
US Micro	6%
International Large	7%
International Small	7%
International Value	7%
Emerging Markets	1%
Emerging Markets Small	1%
Emerging Markets Value	1%
One Year Fixed Income	8%
Short Term Government	4%
Two Year Global Fixed Income	8%
Intermediate Government	4%
Treasury Inflation Protected Securities	2%
Five Year Fixed Income	9%

This chart is for guideline purposes only and is not to be used as actual advice.

The Short Answer:

- **Diversification is the best way to protect your portfolio against risk while still capturing the greatest possible return.**

QUESTION 5

Why Do I Need to Rebalance My Portfolio Periodically?

There are four simple components of successful investing. The previous chapters tackled the first two rules. The third rule of investing is that every investment portfolio should be rebalanced periodically. Rebalancing is critical to ensuring that a portfolio stays on target and suitable to an investor's needs. While rebalancing seems like a simple concept that is easy to accomplish, the reality is that typical investors will not rebalance their portfolios on their own. Most investors make one of two mistakes. They will either ignore their portfolio, which allows their allocation to get out of line, or they do the exact opposite of rebalancing and instead opt to load up on hot sectors and seek to follow yesterday's winners.

Let's assume that you have identified your risk tolerance and you decide on a 50/50 portfolio. This is a portfolio with half of your money invested in equities, or stocks, and the other half in fixed income (treasuries and bonds). You have looked at historical evidence, and you appreciate what you can expect from a portfolio with this mix. You know what history tells us the worst five year period has looked like, and you know how much this portfolio may fluctuate, both up and down, in any given year. Starting from a position with good knowledge and understanding of your downside risk, you are better able to deal with the inevitable market fluctuations. While the past is no guarantee of future performance, you appreciate that a greater mix of fixed income investments has historically been shown to reduce risk, at the cost of decreased returns.

Even though you may begin with a 50/50 mix, your portfolio will probably look different after some time goes by. This is because equities have a higher long-term expected rate of return than fixed income investments. What will likely happen over time is that the equity portion of your portfolio will grow faster than your fixed income portion. If you invested $100,000 at the beginning of the year, you would have started with $50,000 dollars in equities and $50,000 in fixed income. Let's say that at the end of the year, you have grown your portfolio by 10 percent. Now you have a total of $110,000 dollars. However, it's certainly possible that the equities portion could have grown to represent $62,000 dollars, while the fixed income went down to $48,000.

When you started with your 50/50 portfolio, you understood what the risk/reward relationship was for this particular mix. Now at the end of your first year, after equities went up and fixed income went down, your equities now represent about 56 percent of your portfolio and your fixed income only comprises 44 percent. As more years pass, this may drift even further out of alignment.

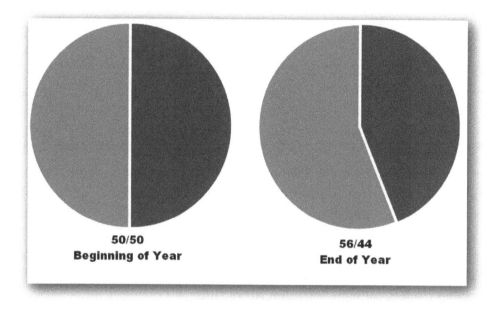

50/50
Beginning of Year

56/44
End of Year

Rebalancing requires that some of the high-flying equities that performed great in the past year be sold and that free money be used to buy the underperforming fixed income. Research has shown that periodic rebalancing is important to long-term investment success and is widely accepted as a prudent tactic. In reality, when it comes time for an investor to actually make the trades necessary to bring the portfolio back in alignment, it's been my experience that instinct often takes over. It feels completely wrong to sell the parts of a portfolio that did well in order to buy more of the investments that underperformed. It's easy to make an excuse about why rebalancing should be ignored this time. It's even easier to look at the returns from the equities portion and want to make more room in the portfolio to chase the hot equity market.

Not all investors keep a close eye on their returns or chase hot sectors in the market. Rebalancing is important even for those investors who simply ignore their portfolios. History tells us that equities will grow at a faster pace than fixed income investments. Over time, a divergence from the original asset allocation of a portfolio will be caused by these increased equities gains. This will be evident in every portfolio, whether closely managed or not. Without rebalancing, it will only take a few years for a portfolio to drift further and further away from what an investor planned, thereby adding a greater level of unanticipated risk to the portfolio.

It is very uncommon for investors to automatically rebalance themselves—whether because it is simply a hard choice to make or because the investors do not watch their portfolios closely enough to know when rebalancing is needed. When a portfolio is correctly rebalanced automatically and periodically by an investment advisor, the portfolio will always maintain the investor's goals. This allows the investor's portfolio to be kept in equilibrium, and his or her objectives are better realized.

The Short Answer:

- **Rebalancing keeps your asset allocation in balance and is needed to prevent your portfolio from drifting away from your suitability and goals over time.**

QUESTION 6

When It Comes to My Advisor, What's the Difference Between a Facilitator and a Fiduciary?

O f all the components I detail to be a successful investor, it is the fourth, having an advisor or coach to keep you on track, that is the hardest for investors to accept as necessary for their overall success. It is also not enough to simply have an advisor. You must choose someone to coach you who is aligned with your investment philosophy. The assistance given by an investment advisor or coach can take two forms: a facilitator or a fiduciary. Which type you work with could be the key to keeping you in line with your investment philosophy and the three other components.

One type of advisor may act as a facilitator. A facilitator is someone who executes your wishes in the way that you ask. For example, you see in your portfolio that US large portion is doing better than international. You meet with your advisor and ask that he or she get you out of the international and invest more in the US large portion. A facilitator will execute your wishes, instead of keeping you diversified or balanced and keeping you on the right path with your investment philosophy. As long as the investment is "suitable," the facilitator has cleared his or her legal burden. You can think of this type of advisor as a pure salesperson.

The other approach is to work with an advisor who is a fiduciary. When advice comes from a professional who follows the fiduciary standard, this person must put your interest above all else, including his or her own. An advisor who follows a fiduciary approach will not willingly let you make investment choices that he or she knows are imprudent or irrational. Going back to the previous example, a fiduciary will coach you through your decision-making process by reminding you about the components of successful investing and keeping your investment philosophy on track. Like a good physician or trusted lawyer, the fiduciary does not confuse giving the clients what they want with giving them what they need. The fiduciary standard is a higher threshold than that of facilitator. Not all advisors are required to follow the fiduciary standard. When working with a professional, the best course of action is to work with someone who has your best interest in the forefront.

DALBAR, Inc., an independent research company, has been studying investor behavior and returns for thirty years. Their study shows that the average investors' returns from their stock portfolios are, on average, a paltry 3.67 percent. Over the same period, the overall market return has been about 10 percent. Why such a disparity? The answer lies mainly with investor behavior. When times are good and the market is headed north, investors are calm and rational. However, when the market turns sour, investors get scared. Emotions take hold, and investors react without regard to common sense or logic. It is in these instances when investors need their coach most. Keeping an irrational investor from diverting his or her sound investment plan at the worst possible time is one of the most important things a coach does. It can mean a big difference in the overall success of your portfolio.

A coach isn't only needed in bad times or down markets. Even when investments look promising, a coach is valuable. During the tech bubble, the media was espousing the apparently never-ending growth potential of technology. They even called it a "new paradigm." With technology stocks posting double digit returns, investors were sucked into euphoria. Some advisors, the facilitators, let their investors jump on the tech bandwagon and didn't prepare them for any downside. The prudent coaches, however, were keeping their flocks steady with a balanced portfolio. Instead of chasing hot sectors, good coaches kept their investors well diversified.

Investing wisely is not complex. It involves being absolutely clear about your investment philosophy and taking actions consistent with that philosophy. A well-crafted portfolio has costs controlled and investments that best harness the highest expected return for a given level of risk. This portfolio would then be left alone, by setting the course and then executing consistently over time. Having the right advisor or coach next to you is your key to keeping all the components together.

The Short Answer:

- **Your investment advisor should have a fiduciary standard— that is, he or she acts with your best interests in mind rather than his or her own.**

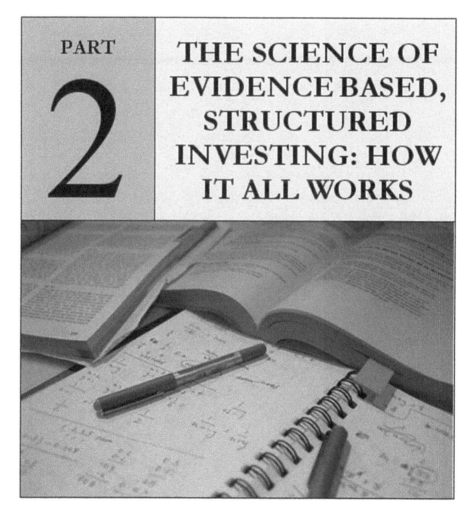

PART

2

THE SCIENCE OF
EVIDENCE BASED,
STRUCTURED
INVESTING: HOW
IT ALL WORKS

QUESTION 7

How Is Wealth Created, and Why Is This Important to Understand?

The creation of wealth is an important concept for investors to understand, as it often fuels the returns in their portfolios. Many people view wealth as how much money someone has, but while wealth and money are related, they are not the same. Wealth is an abundance of economic value, and when we create and trade things of value, we create wealth. When we trade those things of value with others, we in turn create wealth for both parties in the trade. Wealth is not fixed or tangible and has no limits or constraints. It grows naturally out of a healthy, free-market economy. This concept is often difficult to appreciate, yet it's at the foundation of our entire socioeconomic system.

Our economy is vastly larger now than it was merely a century ago. Today, a poor American lives far better than the richest of us lived in the year 1900. At the turn of the century, the average American earned an inflation adjusted wage of $3.43 per hour. Today, the average wage is approximately $12.50 per hour. The average life span has expanded from forty-seven years to seventy-eight years, and the average work week was cut from sixty-six hours per week to just forty hours, according to the US Bureau of Labor Statistics. Are we not wealthier? We all have indoor plumbing, refrigerators, TVs, computers, cars, and cell phones. We can affordably travel by airplane from New York to Los Angeles in five hours. This abundance of additional wealth was created by all the valuable new technology, new inventions, and new services that were created.

A good illustration of the concept of wealth is the creation of the city of New York. Many people are familiar with the history of how the island of Manhattan came to be in the hands of the Dutch. In 1626, the Dutch bought the island from the Native Americans for what today would be equivalent to $1,050. This is not a huge amount of money for what is now some of the most expensive real estate in the world. Hearing this, you might think that the Dutch took advantage of the Native Americans in this deal. But the concept of wealth shows how this is untrue. At the time, the island that would later become Manhattan was worth no more than any other similarly situated piece of land. The land itself, while it had some geographic advantages, was just that—land. It is everything that has happened since the purchase that made Manhattan into what it is today. The creation of the most important city in the world came not from the land, but from the hard work and ingenuity of the millions and millions of people who have called the island home since 1626. All of the streets, the buildings, the subways, the parks, the businesses, and the skyscrapers were created by these people, and in creating the city, these people also created enormous wealth.

One of the worst ideas that affect public policy, both at home and around the world, is that wealth is somehow a zero-sum game. Some think it's like a pizza. If you take a slice of wealth with pepperoni, then there is one less slice available for the rest of us. Many misguided commentators feel that if the rich get richer, then they are taking something from the poor. Some argue that if China grows their economy, this is at the expense of Americans. None of this is true, because there is an unlimited amount of wealth that can be created. Socialism, Marxism, Communism, and other short-sighted "-isms" have all been tied to this zero-sum economic thinking. History shows repeatedly and with clarity that when barriers to trade and free exchange are put up, the economy and the people living in it experience a lower standard of living, higher unemployment, and a generally weaker economy.

The basis of capitalism is free markets that are allowed to meet the needs of the public as a whole in order to grow an economy and create better living standards for the citizens. In order to understand this better, we first need to look at the ways in which wealth is created. Two particularly powerful methods to create wealth are from creativity and free trade.

Creativity

Most Americans know of Steve Jobs, cofounder of Apple. He and his team are responsible for many of the electronic innovations we enjoy today. The first widely adopted home computer, the Apple II, was the brainchild of Jobs and his best friend, Steve Wozniak. Up until then, home computers were relegated to hobbyists, who needed to purchase a kit and then put the entire computer together by themselves. Jobs understood that the average consumer had no interest in putting together a computer. Consumers wanted an appliance, like a toaster or TV—take it out and plug it in, and it works. He used his intellect to see what the consumers truly wanted, even before they could articulate the need. He set about to create a product they would want and would happily pay for. This creative innovation launched what is now one of the most profitable companies the world has ever seen. Steve Jobs took an idea and turned it into something of value. Intuitively, we understand that a person who comes up with useful products and services that consumers desire will profit from his or her ideas. The raw material component of a computer is very inexpensive. It's made of metal, plastic, and glass. It is the assembly and organization of those items into a useful product that gives them value. This is the creation of wealth.

Not all wealth creation needs to be with amazing innovations like computers. They can be more ordinary. It could be that the local grocery store figures out how to better organize its inventory and thereby saves money on storage. That is a creative innovation that creates a small amount of wealth for the company. It could be that UPS figures out how to send drivers on better, more efficient routes, saving time and fuel. Often, creativity and innovations are small scale incremental changes. The accumulation of these small innovations over time increases wealth as a whole. It's the large breakthroughs like electricity and human flight that grab our attention, but incremental innovations are just as vital.

Free Trade

Let's say it's the olden days and you are a blacksmith. You are really good at banging your hammer against a hot piece of iron and turning that into useful items, like wagon wheels, chains, and horseshoes. Across the village lives a farmer who grows corn and other vegetables. He is highly skilled at farming and is very efficient at what he does. The blacksmith is not a good farmer, and the farmer knows nothing about how to work with metal. The blacksmith could never grow corn as easily as he could hammer out a horseshoe. The farmer knows that he has more corn than he could ever eat, and what he really needs is to put shoes on his horses so he can get his corn to the market. It's in both of their best interests to trade with each other. Here is the best part; they are both wealthier because they entered into the agreement under free will. Both the farmer and the blacksmith are better off. Wealth is created when the human mind is able to convert its intelligence, learning, experience, and hard work into something of value. We are leveraging economies of scale and efficiency. That leverage is further multiplied by trading with others who do the same thing.

Now that we have a better understanding of how wealth is created and the role of free-market capitalism, we can apply this understanding to the stock and bond markets. Equities, or stocks, are ownership in companies. Companies are entities that consist of people, applying their ideas and knowledge to create value. It is through companies, rather than just individuals, that our modern society applies the concepts of free trade, creativity, and exchange for value. As companies continue to bring value with innovation and trade with consumers or other companies, wealth is created. As investors, we have the opportunity to harness all of this great creativity and wealth creation, simply by owning equities and bonds.

Cost of Capital and the Creation of Wealth

The cost of capital concept is critical to the understanding of how businesses create wealth. When a business looks to offer a product or service to the market, they often need to raise capital beforehand in order to have the funds to create and deliver that product or service. Before a restaurant opens, for example, they need to secure a facility, purchase equipment and fixtures, and make many other purchases before any customers can come to enjoy a meal.

In order to raise the money necessary to open, a business will often get the capital from two likely sources—equity investment or a loan. If the owner of the business invests his or her own money into the venture, he or she is trading his or her cash for equity in the enterprise. If he or she secures a loan from the local bank, they are agreeing to give him or her set amount of money in exchange for a return of that money in the future plus interest. The interest is the cost of borrowing the money. No one would invest in a company if he or she did not expect the investment to grow. In a publicly traded company, the company raises capital by issuing shares of stock. Investors give their money to a company in exchange for the shares. The investors are anticipating that the company will return their investments in the form of price appreciation and dividends. The company understands that the cost of receiving the investments is the dividends that they must pay to shareholders and the appreciation that the stock makes.

These ideas of wealth creation and the cost of capital are important when we are looking at the market and where returns come from. Your success as an investor is reliant on understanding that returns come from the companies in the market itself. Once we appreciate that wealth is created from companies, we can begin to understand the principles that underlie the system, why the market behaves as it does, and how we can have greater peace of mind about how our money is invested.

The Short Answer:

- **Wealth creation and the cost of capital fuel the returns in your portfolio.**

QUESTION 8

How Do I Know if My Portfolio Is Delivering the Best Expected Return for the Amount of Risk I Am Taking On?

Risk and return are always tied to each other. For any given level of risk, there is an expected level of return associated. Similarly, for any given level of expected return, there is an associated risk. The fundamental concept that risk and return are related is part of an investment philosophy called the Modern Portfolio Theory (MPT). This theory on how investors can maximize their returns for the given amount of risk was first described by Nobel Prize winner Harry Markowitz in 1952. Understanding not only the correlation of risk and return, but how to manage your risk, is essential when it comes to investing.

When creating your portfolio, it's easy to want to jump right to what the average returns are on the funds you are considering, but identifying your risk tolerance level should always come first. Risk measures the volatility of your investment and is represented mathematically in your portfolio as standard deviation. Standard deviation quantifies how much a series of numbers varies around its mean, or average, and when it comes to your investments, standard deviation calculates how much you can expect your fund's return to vary from its average. Let's take a fund with an average return of 8 percent per year and a standard deviation of 20. For this particular fund, two-thirds of the time, we can expect the fund's returns to range between -12 percent and 28 percent. To get here, we take the average return of 8 percent, and then add or subtract its standard deviation of 20.

$$8\% - 20 = -12\%$$
$$8\% + 20 = 28\%$$

Standard deviation provides a precise measure of how varied a fund's return has been over a particular time frame, on both the upside and the downside. With this information, you can judge the range of returns your fund is likely to generate in the future—the greater the standard deviation, the greater the risk. It is your risk measurement and also allows you to evaluate how much volatility you can take on. Understanding your volatility means knowing what the downside would look like for your portfolio if and when we experience another 2007-to-2009-type market drop. Going back to the example above, you may like an 8 percent return, but can you handle a -12 percent return? Knowing this information can better prepare you for how much a fund would likely go down and how long it will take to recover.

Now, I want to give you the choice of two similar investments, both with the same average return, but one with a low risk and the other with a higher risk. Obviously, you will always pick the one with the lesser risk or a smaller standard deviation. Therefore, to induce you to purchase an investment that has a higher risk, there must be a promise of a higher return. In other words, an investor needs to be paid something for taking on the additional risk. In order to get a high return, you have to take on more risk. On the other side, if your investment has low or no risk of loss, you have to accept a low return.

While it is true that high-expected return must come with a commensurate high risk, it is not necessarily true the other way around. It does not always mean that a low return investment takes on lower risk. A problem that many investors have is that they are taking on more risk than they realize and certainly more risk than their expected return warrants. Let me give you an example. Assume we are both headed on a trip to the beach in the same car. The reward is the same for the both of us, a visit to the beach. The risk is that we may get into a car accident on the way there. In this car ride to the beach, I am not wearing my seat belt, but you are. Therefore, my risk of being injured is higher than yours is, even though our reward is still the same. A logical person who understands that a seat belt will save you from injury in the event of a car crash will put on the belt to reduce this risk. For main street investors, it is too often the case that they are not wearing their seat belts, and even worse, they have no idea it's even an option.

Even though we know a high return needs to have a higher risk, when asked what would be the perfect investment, most people would still describe something with a high return but without any fluctuations or risk of loss. This, as you know, is not possible. In order to obtain a real rate of return on your money, you would need to put that money at some level of risk. This relationship between risk and expected return is what led to the development of the Markowitz Efficient Frontier.

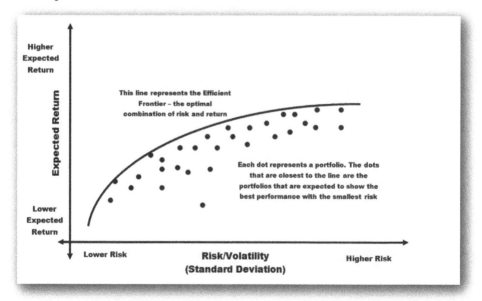

Essentially, there is no investment that can live above the curved line. It simply does not exist. You cannot have a very high return without a very high risk. Understanding this core concept is integral to making the best possible investment decisions. Once you recognize that this curve is our limitation, then the obvious choice is to get as close to the curve as is possible. Where exactly on the curve an investor seeks to place themselves, however, depends in part on the level of risk they are willing to take on.

Managing risk is at the heart of the investing process, though it is not possible to eliminate all risk. It is a simple fantasy to seek a way forward that is without any risk, but even holding cash suffers from the risk of inflation. One common risk that is unmanageable is *systematic risk*. This is the risk that cannot be diversified away. Examples are recessions, interest rate changes, wars, and the like. In 2008, no equity portfolio was immune to the downturn in the market as a result of the great recession. Fortunately, history has shown us that the market has always recovered.

Luckily, there is risk that we can manage, called *specific risk*. This is the risk that a particular stock or group of stocks will underperform. Modern Portfolio Theory explains that balancing out the volatility provides the investor with the best possible return for the given risk. An efficient portfolio is accomplished by managing risk with diversification, blending together the proper mix of assets in the right proportions and keeping the mix consistent over time.

Our understanding of diversification was furthered by the work of Harry Markowitz, William Sharpe, and Merton Miller. Diversification does not mean "own a bunch of different investments," as I gave details about in Question 4. Remember, just owning a lot of stocks, bonds, or mutual funds without an understanding of how the different investments relate misses the mark on maximizing the benefit of diversification. To reduce your risk, diversification is an essential tool.

To illustrate how diversification can help manage risk, let's imagine two investors. Bob owns $500.00 in one large US company. Sally owns the same $500.00 but spread out in 500 different large US companies.

A big concern for Bob is that his one company won't keep up with the market, or worse, it will go out of business. He is figuratively putting "all of his eggs on one basket." Sally, on the other hand, has spread this risk over many companies. If one of the companies Sally invested in goes out of business, she doesn't need to worry because she is still invested in 499 other companies.

Most investors understand this fundamental concept, but unfortunately, this is where it stops. The truth is that the companies in Sally's portfolio are likely to move up and down together; we call this *correlation*. All of the 500 largest US companies tend to move like a flock of birds. Where one goes, they all tend to go. A properly diversified portfolio will have asset classes that don't correlate or have inverse correlation. To make Sally truly diversified, she should invest her $500.00 over different asset classes as well—US large and small, domestic and international, equities and fixed income.

You must remember, assets that move in different directions at different times add a benefit to the investor. Imagine that you could buy two different stocks. When one went up, the other was down, and vice versa. Their relationship to one another aids in keeping the overall investment less volatile than either one can do alone. How do you know how these stocks are going to behave ahead of time? Certain groups of assets, which we call asset classes, tend to move together. An example of an asset class is small US companies, that is, all of the small domestic companies are in one asset class. As one company moves, the others often move similarly based on fluctuations in the market. It's important to realize that each asset class will behave differently over time from another asset class. The most common example of this correlation in the market is when you own both stocks and bonds in a portfolio. Stocks and bonds are separate asset classes because they behave differently as groups. These asset classes move in a different direction from one another at any given time, they do not correlate. Therefore, they are often used together in a portfolio to level out the fluctuations.

Taking this a step further, we also know that spreading our money over a group of large companies and small companies can similarly add diversification because small companies behave differently as a group than larger companies. This is known as asset-class diversification, further explained previously in Question 3. It is really the key to making diversification your buddy. In a properly constructed portfolio, an investor would have about fifteen to twenty separate and distinct asset classes all moving in different directions at any given time. Interestingly, many investment portfolios overemphasize one asset class, that being US large. Indeed, the media speaks to the S&P 500 as if it were the entire market. In truth, it is not, and just owning only large growth companies can lead an investor to significantly underperform a truly diverse portfolio.

20 Asset Classes or More   **2 Asset Classes**

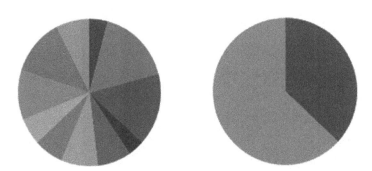

A properly diversified portfolio should own many different asset classes, as illustrated on the left, in order to capture the best expected return for a given level of risk. The portfolio on the right shows what, in my experience, the average investor owns.

While investors often accept the concept of diversification to control their risk, in practice, they do not maintain real diversification. When an asset class is outperforming others, massive amounts of money will move from underperforming asset classes to the high flyer. It seems like investors forget that when funds are having high returns, there is a high risk with achieving it. While diversification is easy to grasp intellectually, in practice, investors are terrible at executing on this simple tenant of good investing and choose to simply chase past returns. We create convenient lies to justify breaking a simple rule to successful investing: staying diversified.

The Short Answer:

- **Standard deviation will help you calculate your risk.**
- **Asset class diversification will help you control your risk.**
- **The Markowitz Efficient Frontier revealed the relationship between risk and return.**

QUESTION 9

In Today's World Where Information Travels at Lightning Speed, How Can Any Investor Gain an Edge?

ost investors I have come across are constantly looking for their next big break—the tip or prediction that will be successful and give them a great return. After seeing countless people fail when these forecasts were not profitable, I knew the truth about the prospects of investors gaining an edge in the market through superior information—they just can't. The typical main street investor has no chance of obtaining an advantage over the market or large financial institutions. Investment firms spend countless millions seeking an advantage over their competition. They install lightning-fast computers and data lines, use the most sophisticated software, and have the best teams available. The traders they employ are smart, aggressive, and come from some of the best universities in the world with advanced degrees in mathematics, statistics, and finance. The average investor could never hope to compete against all of this technological force and manpower.

Today, institutional trading makes up 90 percent of all trades. This means that with all of the millions of trades taking place in the market, average investors make up just 10 percent of them.[2] Chances are that when the average investor purchases a security, the person he or she traded with was not a person at all but actually a large institution. In an efficient market, the price of a stock is the best estimate of its actual value. Only new information can change the price of the stock. This is where institutional advantage comes into play. These companies can receive new information and react on it incredibly quickly—much more quickly than the average investor ever could. This is why trying to compete head on with an institutional trader is a loser's game; they will always be much more prepared to get the best possible price in every single transaction. Statistically, the more you trade against these institutions, the greater your chances of losing, especially when you factor in trading costs. With a 90 percent chance that every trade a person makes is with a superior trader with endless resources, the belief that one can be successful long term is naïve and dangerous.

There is a silver lining to this high volume of institutional trading. An investor does not need to directly compete with the financial machine and can instead harness the benefits of all that competition. When making a trade, professionals at these large institutions work feverishly to win the smallest advantage in the price of the stocks they are buying and selling. In their effort to get the best deal, they are actually creating a more perfect, efficient market, where information is disseminated very quickly to all the participants. Because information travels so quickly in our technological age, this provides the greatest transparency as to the fair value of any given security at any given time.

Over forty year ago, Nobel Laureate Eugene Fama famously unveiled his economic principal known as the Efficient Market Hypothesis. The hypothesis stated that at any given time and in a liquid market, security prices fully reflect all available information and therefore are the best estimate of their fair value. Technology and computers have further leveled the playing field. Because of this, it's difficult, if not impossible, to outperform the market by attempting to locate mispriced securities, time the market, or look to the past as a harbinger of the future. There is substantial evidence that a simple passive indexed fund will outperform most of actively traded funds in any given year. Over a long time period, the advantage is overwhelmingly in the passive investor's favor.

By understanding this, an investor can obtain the greatest expected returns for a given level of risk by largely ignoring the large institutions, hedge funds, and active managers. Investors don't need to play their game, and are not required to compete with them at all. The key to a successful experience with investing is to change your expectations and approach. It begins with a true understanding that active trading does not work and structuring a globally diversified asset class based portfolio is a better long-term approach to investing. It is my belief that by doing so, one is best harnessing the amazing power of the economy in a way that delivers returns matched to risk.

The Short Answer:

- **Technology has made it almost impossible for the main street investor to gain a trading edge over competitors in the market. For those investors who seek to capture market returns, technology has helped make a more robust and efficient market.**

QUESTION 10

Why Does It Seem Like the Market Is Completely Random and Unpredictable?

A casual observer of the stock market, with its roller coaster ups and downs, will certainly notice that the market seems impossible to predict ahead of time. At the close of business today, it is anyone's guess where the market will start tomorrow, because overnight, new information will become known and the price of the securities in the market will reflect this information very quickly. Yet, the 24/7 market news shows have endless "experts" on their broadcasts with logical and well-reasoned predictions of where the market and individual securities are headed. Institutional investment firms take advantage of professional services that are plugged into the news and events as they occur. Still, the advice and predications of the experts not only contradict one another but the market as well. That investors continue to be mesmerized by the endless inconsistent market advice is truly astonishing. As long as there is an audience, the broadcasts will continue.

Unfortunately, the school of evidence leads to a different conclusion. The market reflects the collective decisions of countless investors, both individual and institutional. As new information is made available, the market reflects this in the demand that buyers and sellers place on the supply of securities. It is wholly impossible to forecast where the market is headed ahead of time, based on patterns or other indicators tied into past events.

Two modern economists have made our understanding of the random nature of the market more evident. In 1965, Eugene Fama spoke to this in his academic paper called "Random Walks in Stock-Market Prices." He explains that market prices are completely random and unpredictable, and those purporting to make sense out of historical charts in order to better predict the future are doing nothing more than guessing. Fama's research and ultimate conclusion took a direct shot at the field of technical analysis, comparing their approach to astrology.

Then in 1975, Princeton Professor Burton G. Malkiel wrote a best-selling, consumer-oriented book *A Random Walk Down Wall Street*. In his book, he performs a simple experiment. His students were given a fictional stock that was initially worth fifty dollars. The closing stock price for each day was determined by a coin flip. If the coin flipped heads, the price would close a half point higher, but if the result was tails, it would close a half point lower. Due to just pure odds, each day, the price had a fifty-fifty chance of closing higher or lower than the previous day. Obviously, no historical pattern could be gleaned from this data set. Malkiel then gave the results in the form of a chart to a technical analyst, or a chartist. A chartist is someone who uses charts or graphs of securities' historical prices to attempt to forecast their future trends, essentially looking for well-known patterns to attempt to trade stocks more profitably. The chartist told Malkiel that they needed to immediately buy the stock. Since the coin flips were random, the fictitious stock had no overall trend. The lesson from all of this is that the patterns the analyst saw in the past were purely random and they had no bearing on the future moves.

Countless studies and experiments have been done over the years that essentially came down to the same conclusion. The apparent patterns that emerge in historical data are of little or no value in determining where the market is headed. The market is random and unpredictable because only new and previously unknown information changes the price of a security. Once investors accept that the market is random and efficiently prices new information, they quickly conclude that following the advice of prognosticators is foolhardy. Instead, modern investors, armed with the academic research and empirical evidence, invest scientifically, capturing a broad, diverse basket of securities; rebalance periodically; and avoid unnecessary trading. Doing so over the long term has been shown to provide impressive results.

The Short Answer:

- **No one can consistently predict where the market is headed, because research and empirical evidence has shown that the market is completely random.**

QUESTION 11

Aren't Some Companies Poised to Be Better than Others, and How Do I Figure that Out ahead of Time?

Investing is uncertain. Over time, a number of companies will do better than others. Some will go out of business, some will become the envy of their industry, and many will remain average. Superior returns could surely be earned if one could look at factors present now that could tell us something about the likelihood of success later. While no one can predict which individual companies will skyrocket in the future, we have been able to figure out which asset classes are poised to produce a better expected return.

Research hasn't fully resolved the nature of risk and price movement, but the groundbreaking work of two leading economists sheds new light on the correlation between profit and volatility. Unsatisfied with the incomplete knowledge available, Eugene Fama, a professor at the University of Chicago, and his longtime collaborator Kenneth R. French, a professor at Tufts University, conducted an exhaustive investigation into the sources of risk and return. The result of their research, published in the *Journal of Finance* in 1992, was called "The Cross-Section of Expected Stock Returns."

Fama and French discovered that three factors explain about 95 percent of all returns, and the research laid out in "The Cross-Section of Expected

Stock Returns" has widely come to be known as the Fama-French three-factor model. The model has become the standard for explaining stock pricing and expected returns and forever changed the investment world.

The first factor is the *market factor*. In determining a fair price for a stock, buyers and sellers must assess the risk in a particular asset and compare that risk to the market as a whole. The most widely known model is the capital asset pricing model, or CAP-M. CAP-M examines the volatility of an individual stock in relation to the market as a whole, assigns the additional volatility (a factor called beta), and assumes that stocks will be priced to reflect both market risk and the particular risk of the individual stock. CAP-M and beta are brilliant and elegant concepts, but they don't give the complete picture. The market factor explains about 70 percent of returns. If a stock is up by 10 percent for the year, about 70 percent of that can be explained by CAP-M.

The second factor is the *size factor*. Different size companies have different levels of risk and commensurately, different expected returns over time. Small companies are riskier than large ones, but they also have a better historic rate of return. According to Ibbotson Associates, the annualized annual rate of return of small US companies from 1926 to 2005 is 12.6 percent. For the same period, large companies in the United States had a 10.4 percent return. This 2.2 percent difference may not seem substantial, but over time, with compounding, the impact to an investment is impressive.

The different levels of return are explained by the fact that small companies that are less established tend to be riskier and their prices more volatile. Investors get a relative discount when they buy stock in these companies, to compensate for that risk. This discount allows the stock of small companies to outperform large companies in the long run.

To say this another way, imagine you have the choice to invest in a basket of large, robust blue chip companies that have shown the ability to weather the ups and downs of the market or a group of smaller companies without the size to absorb market fluctuations and other factors. Which would you choose? The answer would probably depend on what they cost. If both stocks were offered at the same price, most would take the safer investment. Why would we want to put our capital at a greater risk without getting something better in return? The market realizes that in order for a person to purchase a small company's riskier stock, the person would need to purchase the stock at a cheaper price. This lower relative purchase price is the reward for taking on the greater risk. Under this scenario, we can see that the risk of owning the smaller company is rewarded through greater returns.

The third factor is known as the *value factor*. Companies can be divided up into categories called growth or value. Companies with a high book-to-market ratio are value companies, which means they are "cheap," as compared to other companies that are trading at a relatively low book-to-market ratio. The book-to-market ratio is the value of a company's assets, fixtures, equipment, and buildings in comparison to the market value of their stock. Growth companies are typically healthy, well run companies. Value companies are the opposite of growth companies; they are companies that are distressed or might need some fixing. A higher book-to-market ratio means that the market sees a reason to keep their share price relatively low.

Not surprisingly, value companies are riskier. But Fama and French found that these value companies also had a commensurately higher level of expected return. This makes sense. Similar to the previous two factors, risk must be rewarded; otherwise, no one would take on the added risk.

Compare my ability to play the piano with Billy Joel's. I am a terrible piano player; I can't play anything. Billy Joel, of course, is the "Piano Man." No one is going to dispute that he is better at playing the piano than I am, but at the same time, I have a much greater degree of potential improvement. Billy is already playing at a near perfect level. No matter how much he practices, he will only make marginal improvements. However, I have so much potential to improve. If I were to hire a teacher and practice, I would surely get much better. If Billy Joel and I were companies, I would be a value company and he would be a growth company, because value companies have much more room to improve and as a group they tend to exhibit a higher level of return over time.

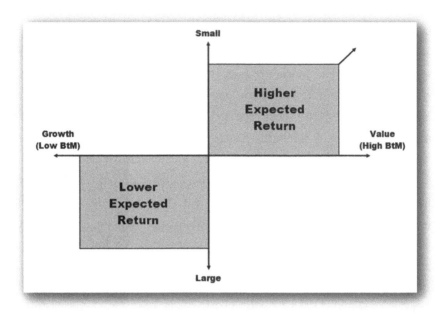

The graph above illustrates the relationship between higher risk and future expected return. The top right quadrant represents stocks with the highest expected return, but also the highest volatility. The lower left quadrant shows stocks with the least volatility, but a lower expected return.

In structuring a world-class portfolio, investors can match up their risk tolerance with the best possible expected rate of return by employing the three-factor model. This science, combined with the concepts of the Efficient Market Hypothesis, and Modern Portfolio Theory, has helped main street investors capture market returns without the need to speculate and gamble with their hard-earned money.

The Short Answer:

- **The Fama-French three factor model has shown why certain asset classes have a greater expected return than others.**

PART 3

SPECULATING AND GAMBLING WITH YOUR MONEY: WHAT WE KNOW DOES NOT WORK

QUESTION 12

I Like to Pick My Own Companies; Why Doesn't Stock Picking Work?

The process of attempting to select a stock that will outperform others is a popular investment strategy. A popular method for selecting stocks is through doing actual research into companies and looking into their fundamentals in order to find mispriced securities. Another method, more common with average investors, is simply picking out a few companies one knows or likes. However, no matter which method is used to select the individual securities, stock picking is not the key to successful investing.

Fundamental analysis is the laborious process of delving deep into all of the available information about a company in order to find the true value of that company. This means the investor would look behind the curtain and research the basics about the company in order to see how it stacks up with what the market says it is worth. They would look at the management team, business prospects, profits, losses, cash flow, debts, expenses, and other fundamentals of the business in an effort to ascertain what the true value of the company should be.

When that value is different from what the stock market has priced the security, there is an opportunity to make a profit from the mispricing. Let's say, for example, your analysis determines that a company is worth $100.00 per share, but the market has it priced at $50.00. The shrewd investor will want to invest in this underappreciated gem, and when the market eventually catches up to what he or she already knows, the price will rise accordingly. This investor believes he or she will profit from his or her superior ability to ascertain the best stocks poised for future appreciation. This logical, commonsense approach is appealing on many levels. Our sense of fairness and desire to reward hard work conforms to our notion that fundamental analysis should be successful.

Followers of fundamental analysis keep a good amount of common sense on hand. They point out that investors can be lazy, emotional, and irrational and don't look at the facts. They are trying to separate the real value from hype and unsubstantiated exuberance. On paper, fundamental analysis makes sense. The issue, however, is that in the modern day, there are surprisingly few examples of investors applying this technique to consistently outperform the market as a whole.

In the 1970s, and before, when information was not as readily available as it is now, I can see how an investor with superior training and information could ferret out the companies that were underpriced. Back then, the technology to disseminate information was far more rudimentary. For many people, their method of obtaining new business information was the daily paper and nightly newscast. Today, it's a totally different story. A celebrity can write a post on Facebook, and within five minutes, a million people have viewed and "liked" it. News that affects the markets travels even faster, with entire enterprises geared up to take advantage of new information instantaneously. It seems very implausible that an average investor armed with fundamental analysis could estimate the true value of an individual stock better than the rest of the market.

Worse yet, some investors do not bother with any type of analysis at all. They would rather choose to buy companies based solely on the fact that they know them or like them and their products. Buying a company just because of familiarity or proximity is one of the biggest mistakes an investor can make. Will Coca-Cola have a better return than Pepsi, just because you think Coke tastes better? People also buy companies because they believe in them or their message. The truth is that a company's mission statement has no effect on its long-term prospects. Over time, similar companies in the same asset class will have the same expected return.

Terrance Odean studied investor trading in his 1997 paper "Do Investors Trade Too Much?" He followed ten thousand random accounts from a nationwide discount brokerage house and their trades from 1987 to 1993. His research found that the average return investors obtained on securities they bought was less than the return on the securities they sold. The securities they bought were underperforming the ones the investors sold. Even more startling results showed that over one sample year securities purchased had an average 3.3 percent lower return than those sold. His research has shown us that stock picking is not improving an investor's return.

At the end of the day, all of the very experienced traders with access to all of the new and relevant information create a robust market that is the best estimate of the value of a company at any one time. With modern day technology, it is almost impossible for one person to have information that is not available to all other investors. The average investor has as much chance of beating the market over twenty years as flipping a coin to heads every time twenty times in a row. Stock picking is not a solution. Owning equities (with fixed income), diversifying globally, and rebalancing your portfolio while working with an investment coach are essential components to focus on to be a successful investor.

The Short Answer:

- **Picking individual companies has not been shown to produce higher returns than simple indexing, and making stock selections based on your personal feelings will likely increase risk while decreasing returns in your portfolio.**

QUESTION 13

I Like to Get In and Out of the Market to Avoid Downturns; Why Doesn't Market Timing Work?

Watching the destruction of an investment portfolio as the market takes a slide is difficult for many to endure. An investor who is nearing retirement may feel that he or she cannot afford to watch his or her entire savings evaporate in a market downturn. This investor rationalizes the need to cash out before his or her entire portfolio is gone. When an investor seeks to jump in and out of the market or a sector of the market as prices rise and fall, it is called *market timing*. In the midst of a dip in the market, logic and patience are at a minimum, and investors might not realize that by liquidating to cash, they are "locking in" their losses. Investors never complain when the market is up and everything seems rosy. When returns are climbing, investors are very interested in staying fully invested. But when the market has appeared too good to be true and then begins to drop, the itch for market timing is especially prevalent.

The market drop that took place between 2007 and 2009 is a prime example. The news media and experts were overwhelmingly pessimistic. The firestorm was all-consuming. Stories of bank failures, drastic employer layoffs, and overall doom filled the nightly news. The comparison was to the Great Depression. By March of 2009, when the US market hit rock bottom and then began its long ascent, few believed that a recovery was sustainable. The commentary was that it was a momentary upturn prior to another major leg down.

Many believe that the experienced financial professionals who work on Wall Street will be able to predict the best times to get in and out of the market. Surely, a hands-on approach, actively looking ahead and navigating, would give a better overall return with far less risk than a simple buy-and-hold approach. However, one of the biggest mistakes of all is the belief that it's possible to successfully market time. Market timing is in actuality nothing more than gambling, whether it is you or your financial advisor who is placing the bets.

The path that the market will take tomorrow is wholly unknowable, because the events of tomorrow have yet to unfold. This means that in the short run, prices are constantly in flux, twisting, turning, and gyrating without a pattern and the market has no memory. This is known as the random walk hypothesis. According to Eugene Fama, market timing is a flimsy dangerous occupation.

Part of the problem with market timing as a strategy is that the investor needs to be right way more than he or she is wrong. It's not as simple as being right at least 50 percent of the time, as some mistakenly believe. What needs to be appreciated is that the long-term trend of the market is upward. If the average return of the total market is in the neighborhood of 10 percent per year, then sitting in cash for any of this time means that you are not garnering that return. If you pull out while the market is headed north, you have guaranteed that you can never make up for that mistake.

Professor William Sharpe set out to determine how often a market timer must be correct to beat a simple market index. In his 1975 study, "Likely Gains from Market Timing," Sharpe concluded that the market-timers must be correct 74 percent of the time in order to outperform a passive portfolio of similar risk. Other studies have confirmed his conclusion.

In reality, the market timing professionals are not coming close to this mark. According to the independent advisory group CXO, the average investment gurus they studied have 47 percent accuracy—their guesses are not even right half the time.

Further, the cost imposed by the system of all this trading is yet an additional headwind that needs to be overcome. We will discuss costs in another chapter, but make no mistake; the costs of trading are a major reason why active market picking is destined for failure. It is widely known that the trading cost of the average actively traded fund is around 2 to 4 percent per year. This means that the market timers have to be that much better just to stay even. Even if you think you are buying and holding, often, the manager you are employing is using market timing activities inside your mutual fund portfolio. So unless you truly understand what is going on in your fund, you may very well be timing the market.

Where this leaves us is with substantial evidence that the likely result of attempted is a reduction in expected return and an increase in risk. The investors who understand the folly of trying to game the system and simply invest consistently with their risk tolerance do achieve greater expected returns and peace of mind. Through education, one can understand that returns do not come from timing the market but instead, harnessing the wealth creating attributes of equities over the long term.

The Short Answer:

- **There is no clear evidence that market timing works consistently or predictably; it's a better choice to stay invested for the long term.**

QUESTION 14

I Like to Invest Only in the Areas of the Market that Seem to Be on the Rise. Why Shouldn't I Chase Hot Sectors?

I n 2014, the S&P 500 outperformed almost every other asset class that year. The news reports were saying that the market was breaking all-time records. Educated investors know statements like those are misleading. The S&P 500 is not the entire market; it's only five hundred companies out of thousands of companies that make up the whole market. Even though the large US companies had exceptional returns in one particular year, it does not mean that the entire market has been up or was breaking records.

When one sector is outperforming the rest of the market, it is common for investors to ask that more of their portfolio be invested in that portion to ride the wave. Doing so is called *track record investing* or chasing hot sectors, and the evidence is that this type of investing does not work. Since no one can predict the future, no one can predict the market. There is always going to be a hot sector or asset class at any given time, and the news will always widely report on it in absolute terms. If in one year, it's the S&P 500, the chances are slim it will repeat the next year because the market has no memory; it only looks forward. Tomorrow, it may be real estate, technology companies, international companies, gold, or US micro stocks. No one knows what will outperform expectations in the future, which is why chasing the hot asset class and market segments does not lead to long-term success.

We can all recall the technology run-up from the late 1990s. At that time, the tech-heavy NASDAQ composite was breaking all-time records. According to Morningstar, by March 2000, it peaked at about 5,000 points, before dropping like a rock to about 1200 points. It took about fifteen years for the NASDAQ to recover that previous peak. Investors should have learned an important lesson from that. However, investors have what is sometimes called a "recency bias" and therefore tend to shortsightedly focus on the recent past and assume that the future will follow accordingly.

A good way to illustrate this concept is to look at how the S&P 500 has performed over a longer term. Despite its popularity, US large has not been the best asset class over time. Based on data derived from the Center for Research & Security Pricing, from 1973 to 2013, US large has delivered about 10.27 percent. Yet US small has given us 12.92 percent. If you invested $100,000.00 in 1973, it would have grown to an impressive $5.5 million if invested in US large. Even more impressive would be if you had invested in US small, for that same investment would have grown to an astonishing $14.6 million. The annual compounding of the interest over time means that a relatively small difference in annual interest rate growth means an impressive difference in real returns.

With that being said, it's not recommended that you invest all of your money in US small value, US large growth, or any other particular asset class, because with less diversification comes greater volatility. So while time is our friend, having all investments in any one sector or asset class can be extremely risky. The approach that balances this is asset class diversification, as we discussed in Question 4. Chasing the hot sector, no matter how attractive the returns appear in the short term, is dysfunctional investment behavior that violates the basic rules of investing and often re-sults in investors being forced to accept greater risk and lackluster returns.

The Short Answer:

- Track record investing or chasing hot sectors of the market has not been shown to work better than investing in a simple pas-sive broad based index fund.

QUESTION 15

What Are the Costs Associated with Investing? Are There Hidden Costs in My Portfolio?

U nderstanding the costs in your investment portfolio is a key step to obtaining greater peace of mind. So much of how investors view their portfolio success comes down to only what they see on their statements. Investors focus only on the stated expenses, assuming that if it's not disclosed, it does not exist. This is not true. Undisclosed fees and costs are one of the dirty secrets of the investment industry. Costs come in a variety of forms, and they are often hidden from view. Common sense tells us that all things being equal, an investment with fewer costs will outperform the higher cost alternative. These costs can be viewed as a headwind that the investor needs to cut through in order to achieve the best possible returns.

Disclosed Fees

For a traditional mutual fund, the management fee of the fund itself is called the expense ratio. This operating expense is the fee paid to a fund's investment managers and also includes other costs, like recordkeeping, custodial services, taxes, legal expenses, and accounting and auditing fees.

Depending on the type of fund, operating expenses vary widely. Some funds have a marketing cost referred to as a 12b-1 fee, which would also be included in operating expenses. However, a fund's trading activity, the buying and selling of portfolio securities, is not included in the calculation of the expense ratio.

According to a 2013 Morningstar report, the average US mutual fund has a reoccurring expense ratio of about 1.26 percent. For international funds, it's 1.43 percent. This means that each and every year, the investor needs to pay the manager this fee for maintaining the fund. Some costs are inevitable. Managing a mutual fund is an incredibly complex undertaking requiring substantial manpower and technological effort. There is no such thing as a free lunch, but costs should always be limited to those that are necessary and reasonable.

Some funds also charge an upfront fee, often referred to as a load. This is essentially a cost to get into the investment and is largely as sales commission. It pays the broker or middleman for recommending the fund. However, not all funds charge a load. I recommend that investors never use a fund that charges a load, because historically these funds have not shown to perform any better than funds without the charge, so it's essentially a waste of your money.

Some other funds charge a special fee to sell the fund. This is called a contingent deferred sales load (CDSL), or back-end load. This is a real masterpiece of the mutual fund deception. The only purpose of a back-end load is to confuse investors and make them think they are buying a no-load fund when they are not. A CDSL is simply a full load in disguise. Instead of imposing a sales fee up front, this type of fund will eliminate the front-end load entirely but impose an exit fee if a shareholder leaves the fund in the first year. This exit fee will decrease each year. Usually, funds that charge back-end loads are called "class B" shares, and often, after the end of five years, they will convert into class A shares. A CDSL fund will also charge investors a 12b-1 marketing fee each year.

One final load investors should be aware of is the level load. This type of load usually charges about 1 percent in 12b-1 fees each and every year you are invested. These types of shares are often designated as "class C" shares. Though there is no up-front or back-end load, the level load ends up being the most expensive type of load for a long-term shareholder. The level load will continue for as long as you hold the fund, draining away your money over time.

Hidden Fees

Hidden costs can do just as much damage to your returns as the disclosed variety can. One type of cost that investors might not be aware of or see directly on their statement is explicit trading costs or brokerage commissions. These costs exist because the act of selling a share of a security held in the fund incurs a sales commission. The average fund has a turnover of 88 percent. This means that if a mutual fund held one hundred different companies on January 1, the manager of the fund has sold eighty-eight of them and bought new companies by the end of the year. The commissions produced through all of this activity are substantial. This generates revenue for the brokerage firm while reducing the returns to an investor. Funds that are actively traded will always have greater turnover than those that follow a buy-and-hold approach. Investors can save themselves substantial costs by appreciating that active funds do not make up the cost of all this trading with superior results. In the end, the investor pays for all of the trading the fund manager did, at the cost of their return.

In addition to the hidden costs are implicit costs that are not reported anywhere and can only be estimated. They take the form of the bid-ask spread and the market impact costs. The bid-ask spread is similar to a commission and takes the following form. At any given time, the price of a security purchased will be slightly greater than what it can be sold for. Thus, if a stock is fifty dollars to purchase, then it may be something like $49.50

to sell. That difference in price is a form of sales commission paid to the market makers who are in charge of matching up the buyers and the sellers. Just like the overt sales commission from above, the more trading done in a portfolio, the greater the costs to the investor. Generally, investors who buy and hold in a diversified portfolio do better than those who incur a lot of trading, in part because of the bid-ask costs. A study by William J. Bernstein, a respected authority in the field of financial economics, estimates that the bid-ask spread can add between .3 and 3.0 percent to the cost of each trade.

The last implicit cost to investors is the market impact. Based on the laws of supply and demand, when securities are sold, they put downward pressure on the price of the investment. Similarly, as buyers seek to purchase securities, there is an upward force placed on the share price. If a stock is currently selling for $100 per share and an investor wants to sell a large block of shares in the open market, then someone will need to buy them. However, there may not always be enough interested investors willing to purchase the shares, so the seller needs to make the offer sweeter. This takes the form of a lower price. After the trade, the price rebounds back to its equilibrium price. This is known as the market impact cost, and it's yet another invisible cost that investors pay. The best way to avoid or reduce this cost is to limit your investment to funds that follow a structured buy-and-hold approach. Once the security is acquired, it is typically held for a long time, and unnecessary costs are avoided.

Investors who are aware of costs and attempt to control them have shown to outperform investors who ignore the detrimental impact of unmanaged expenses. It's important for investors to realize that just because you can't always see expenses on your quarterly statement, that does not mean that they are not hidden and slowly siphoning away your return. While some costs are inevitable and should be expected, investors should work with a professional trained to see the entire picture. It is only then

that one can appreciate all of the relevant facts and acquire the most suitable investments possible.

The Short Answer:

- **Costs, both disclosed and hidden, should be limited to those
that are reasonable and warranted because the impact of heavy
unnecessary costs to a portfolio is substantial.**

QUESTION 16

Why Isn't Gold a Good Investment Choice?

There are many people who believe gold is a sound investment for their portfolio. I am not one of them. Gold, while a very important commodity to our modern life, does not in and of itself do anything.

Investing involves a concept known as the "cost of capital," as we discussed in Question 7. If I give my money to a company in exchange for shares in that company, then my reward is that in the future, I get to keep a portion of value of that company and its profits. This reward may come in the form of dividends or appreciation in the price per share. There is a cost to the company for ac cepting my investment. They don't get my money for free; they need to pay me something for the use of it. Similarly, if I buy a certificate of deposit at the local bank, there is a cost to the bank for using my money. That cost is the interest rate on the CD. This cost of capital is at the heart of investing, and understanding this concept helps flush out real investments from speculation and gambling.

The cost of capital concept does not exist with gold, or any other commodity for that matter. Gold has no untapped intrinsic value. It is worth only what people are willing to pay for it. After all, the gold itself does not do anything. It's just a metal that sits in a vault at a bank or in your back yard in a tin can, until it is traded to someone else. While it is true that gold is used in industry, it is just a raw material. Thus, trading in gold is not investing; it is just speculating. Its price is only related to the laws of supply and demand. The person selling you gold is merely selling you one hard asset (cash) for another (gold).

The second reason gold does not make sense as an investment is less theoretical and more practical. The long-term return of gold is terrible. In fact, the long-term return on an ounce of gold is only slightly better than inflation. Over the past two hundred years, after adjusting for inflation, $10 invested in gold would have a real return of $26. On the other hand, that same $10 invested in the stock market would have turned into about $5,600.[3] The only people who have really made money on the recent gold craze have been the facilitators, processors, and fly-by-night dealers. I always found it amusing that the very people telling you to buy gold now are trading you their gold for your cash.

The actual buyers are taking on a huge risk and are not getting an appropriate level of return to compensate them for this risk. We know from investing that every return has a relationship to risk. From 1836 to 2011, the real rate of return of gold has been 1.1 percent with a standard deviation (volatility/risk) of 13.1. This is a bad deal for the buyer. It means that the returns are small and the volatility is relatively high. By way of comparison, an asset with a similar rate of return is US treasuries. The real rate of return of for US treasury bills from 1973 to 2013 is 0.90, while the standard deviation is 3.41.[4] If you look at these numbers, you can see that gold had a similar return but the risk was much higher.

Many investors want the risk of treasuries and the returns of the stock market. In truth, when buying gold, you're more likely to take the risk of stocks with the returns of a T-bill. I do not believe that gold has a place in an investment portfolio, except for the gold-mining companies that are in the business of extracting it from the ground and refining it for a profit.

The Short Answer:

- **Gold is a poor choice for a diversified portfolio because it has no intrinsic value and has been shown to have high volatility with low potential long-term returns.**

QUESTION 17

Why Aren't Indexed Annuities a Good Option for My Portfolio?

At first glance, the promise of the equity-indexed annuity is appealing. It claims that you get the upside of the stock market without the risk of the downside or volatility. Well, of course, who would not love this pitch? Yet, the devil is in the details. If you do a Google search of "equity-indexed annuity scams," approximately 65,000 hits are produced (as of this writing). These products are often sold to retirees with the promise that they are a safe way to participate in the market. In my experience, however, the returns are in the 2 to 3 percent range *and* your money is locked up for long periods. These aren't the only issues that I see with equity indexed annuities.

One of my other big concerns with these annuities is that they are very complicated insurance-based products. As a practicing lawyer, I am trained and experienced in reading and deciphering complicated contracts. Even I find these instruments particularly confusing. If a trained professional finds it difficult to understand these agreements, how can an average investor do better? When I ask people if they understand their annuity, I usually only get the good parts from them—that is, that they won't lose their investment. They do not understand or know the complexity of the product they bought.

Now, let's say you have gone through the contract and it has been fully explained to you how the annuity actually works. You then find out that they do not let you participate in any of the dividends distributed from the equities you are tracking. A common type of annuity is one indexed to the S&P 500. When the five hundred largest US companies, which make up the S&P 500 index, issue dividends, this means you are not credited with any of those distributions. The annuity company keeps the dividends as opposed to passing them along to you.

Another issue that I find with these annuities is a concept called a market cap. What this means is that although the returns of the market are very high in a particular period, you are capped at a certain maximum for the year. Go back to this S&P 500 indexed annuity. This annuity you have may have a maximum market cap at say 7 percent. In 2014, the S&P 500 was up by about 25 percent—yippie! But when you get your statement in the mail, why don't you see a 25 percent return on your investment? Your returns were capped at 7 percent, regardless of how high the returns reached in the S&P 500. Like with the dividends, the excess returns stay with the annuity company.

Most of these contracts also have something called a participation rate. This means that you only participate in a percentage of the upside returns. This is separate from the market cap I explained above. For instance, assume that the market was up 6 percent for the year. Your market cap is 7 percent, so you get all of this 6 percent, right? You may not get the full 6 percent return; rather, you are only allowed to participate in say 75 percent of that upside. You will only be credited with a return of about 4.5 percent (0 .75 times 6 percent). Again, the annuity company keeps the difference.

Finally, the commissions paid to the insurance salespeople who peddle these instruments are very lucrative. In many cases, they earn an immediate 6 to 10 percent fee for selling annuities to the investor. Investing $100,000.00 in an annuity would provide the insurance salesperson $6,000.00 to $10,000.00 immediately as commission. While you don't necessarily see your money being used to pay commission on your statement, the investors are then asked to wait years to get back their principal and hope for a return. I have seen annuity contracts with a sixteen-year term and an 18 percent surrender penalty. Having investors, especially seniors, wait sixteen years to have full access to their principal is unconscionable. Many states have enacted consumer protection laws to protect the public from overzealous or unscrupulous salespeople.

Nothing is free. We know there are costs in all investment tools, which I further detail in Question 15. Annuity companies are in business to make money, just like any other company. Their complicated contracts, with caps and restrictions that investors rarely learn about or understand, are what make me cringe. It has been my experience that while you are not likely to lose your principal in one of these complicated contracts, chances are you are not going to be happy with your meager annual returns of about 2 to 3 percent. Folks are constantly asking me what I think about indexed annuities. My answer is always the same: don't buy them.

The Short Answer:

- **Indexed annuities are often misleading and complicated; they have not been shown to provide investors with the anticipated returns and are not an alternative to a diversified market portfolio.**

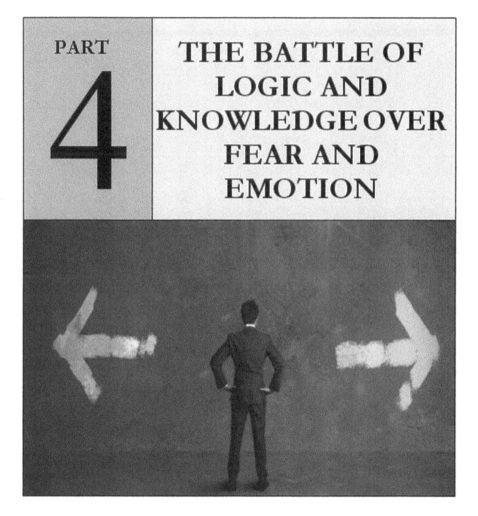

PART

4

THE BATTLE OF LOGIC AND KNOWLEDGE OVER FEAR AND EMOTION

QUESTION 18

I Know the Market Is Due for a Correction. Don't I Need to Protect My Nest Egg?

Every time the economy goes into a recession or the market corrects, we often hear a common refrain: "I can't afford to lose all of my money." It certainly happened in 2000–2002 and in 2007–2009. Both of these very serious recessions ushered in a panic for investors. In the media, on Bloomberg, CNBC, and Fox Business, many so-called experts sounded off on just how bad the crash was going to be. They all agreed that this time it was *really* different. I can remember a certain outspoken host from CNBC, predicting during the 2007 crash that when people went to use the ATM, no money would come out. Another frequent guest on these shows, who writes books on what he sees as trends in the market, told us in January of 2009 that we were headed into the next great depression. He even advised people to sell all their stocks and buy US treasuries. This advice was clearly bad, and listening to him would have meant that investors would have missed one of the strongest bull runs in recent history. This sort of exaggeration multiplies our natural fear. It is perfectly normal to be fearful when the market drops. It is how we react to this information, however, that sets a successful investor apart from the others.

The truth is that it's *always* different. Each and every sustained drop in the market is caused by different factors. The most recent drop was widely attributed to banks issuing collateralized debt obligations that they did not understand, along with lenders issuing mortgages to people who were underqualified. In the 2000–2002 bear market, technology companies were being traded at higher and higher prices, until investors determined that the value of these companies did not match up with the prospects for their future. The crash of 1987 was caused by something entirely different as well and so on and so on. No two crashes are alike, because each is caused by completely different circumstances that cannot be predicted. Chances are that the next bear market will be caused by something that is wholly unapparent to us today. There is simply no way to know.

What we have witnessed, over the past century and going back even further, is that businesses and people are able to adapt to a new environment in a surprisingly short amount of time. Earnings and profits have always returned, because the stock market reflects the health of the companies that it comprises. In the past eighty-plus years, the market has corrected more than eighty-five times, with about twenty bear markets. It has typically taken the market just above four months to come back to pre-correction levels.[5] What does this mean for investors? Like we have seen in the past, there will always be numerous small bumps along the way, along with a few large bumps. Investors need to keep in mind that after each bump, the market has quickly recovered, with the economy often following suit. Historically, it's been immediately after a correction or a crash that the highest rates of return are earned. Those who panic and sell off at the bottom or on the way down often lock in their losses, only to miss out on the sharp recovery that occurs soon thereafter.

The smart investor is the one who stays in the game, rides out each crash, and then reaps the rewards of his or her patience and consistency during the market's recovery. The most important thing to understand is that while each crash truly is different, each recovery is remarkably the same. It's been my experience that investors who do not have a trusted advisor to turn to in these instances of panic and turmoil are subject to the greatest likelihood to veer of course. Without the calm reassurance of someone who is trained to answer your call, you will more than likely sell at the bottom, thereby inflicting the greatest possible damage to your portfolio. On the other hand, those who have a plan to deal with inevitable drops, those who have thought ahead and decided that they want someone in their corner to guide them when things look bleak—these investors are almost always long-term winners.

The Short Answer:

- **No one knows when the next market correction will occur, but successful long-term investors ignore short-term market predictions and instead hold a long-term view.**

QUESTION 19

I Am Afraid of Losing All of My Money, Why Do I Need To Invest in the Market at All?

Although the market has been on the rise in recent years, people are still scared from the 2007 crash. Many people lost a significant chunk of their investments and were not prepared to see the loss on their statements as the market hit its lowest point. As a result, many chose to pull their money from the market and go home. With no confidence that they had a chance to recover those losses, many investors relegated themselves to meager interest rates on CDs and money market accounts at the local savings bank. Others fell victim to fixed-indexed annuities, with too good-to-be-true promises of both great returns and total protection from market loss.

Unfortunately, it has been my experience that CDs and other guaranteed insurance products don't provide the returns necessary to keep pace with inflation. It is inflation, or reduction in buying power, that can ultimately cost investors the most. Investors who demand safety might not realize that what they are ultimately doing is going broke slowly.

The financial meltdown is still fresh in American minds, and from what I've seen, many investors have lost faith in the system. There is plenty of blame to go around and so many examples of firms and rogue traders acting badly. It is surprising that so few criminal prosecutions have come from what appeared to be widespread abuse of the financial system. In a recently published survey, well over 90 percent of respondents felt that Wall Street needs further regulations to keep the public safe.[6]

This puts middle-class Americans in a difficult spot. On the one side is an industry that appears complex and volatile. On the other is the insufficient interest offered by the local savings banks and large insurance companies. Some people will choose to invest, all the while fearing that the system is taking advantage of them and not delivering the best returns to their portfolio. Others will stick to CDs and worry about their investments slowly eroding over time.

However, with a bit of an education, an investor can find some comfort. Investing in the market can be done in a way that avoids the risk of loss associated with Wall Street's bad actors. And while no equity portfolio was immune from the 2007 slide, a well-designed, globally diversified portfolio that avoids actively managed funds will insulate an investor from much of this potential loss. It all goes back to the philosophy by which you are investing your money.

If you employ a passive or structured approach that seeks to hold a very large, diverse basket of investments, you are avoiding the very game they want you to play. A buy-and-hold strategy means that investments will be in your portfolio for as long as you stay invested and there is very limited selling. Further, the diversification offered by holding thousands of unique securities means that the bad acts of a few do not budge your long-term trajectory.

An investor is best equipped to deal with the concerns of Wall Street greed by working with an investment advisor or coach trained in the science of prudent investing. The advisor's job is to explain what we know to be the truth—where returns come from and how to harness the amazing wealth creation engine of our modern economy. A well-trained advisor can show his or her client why investing for the long term in a globally diversified portfolio is far superior to the fear-driven options that investors typically want to employ, like buying gold bars or guaranteed annuities. These "safe" investments may seem like a solution to gain greater peace of mind, but they create a new, bigger, and real problem of locking investors into a future of going broke safely.

The Short Answer:

• **Equities are one of the best wealth creation tools available. Ownership in equities allows investors to outpace inflation.**

QUESTION 20

How Does the Media Derail My Investment Peace of Mind?

I n today's technologically advanced society, the media can broadcast the latest news almost immediately and through many different means. You can log on to any news website for up-to-the minute information or even get notifications sent directly to the smartphone in your hand. The media will often focus their offerings toward what consumers find compelling. In its simplest form, human nature drives us to respond to tragic events, especially as they are unfolding. You know the common saying, "If it bleeds, it leads." The competitive nature of the media business means that they will sensationalize their content to keep consumers plugged in, whether it's the latest snowstorm predictions or a tragic accident. What consumers watch or read about investments is put there to sell newspapers or get people to tune in, not because it is the most accurate picture of current market conditions.

There are countless media outlets that focus solely on the stock market and investing. Just like with any other news channel, these outlets are not interested in giving you investment peace of mind. They have no economic incentive to put shows on the air about the wisdom of a slow-and-steady, well diversified, passively constructed portfolio. A diversified portfolio, while very successful, would make a pretty boring news story. It does not chase the hot sector or follow the latest trends. Viewers are far more inter-ested in hearing stories about a new company that just went public, how some lucky investors made a killing on the run-up, or the latest projections about where the US economy is headed.

The content the media pushes out is designed to keep investors tuned in, even if it could cause potentially destructive investment behavior. On networks like CNBC, Fox Business, and Bloomberg News, they air non-stop shows about the market, money, and trading. Most are the straight-forward market-watch variety, where the only job for the host and guests is to comment on the day's activities, along with making predictions about the future. These shows exploit our emotions. They create a sense that an investor needs to make changes to his or her portfolio in order to best maximize returns or avoid another market crash. This creates a vicious cycle—the more that you watch or consume, the more you act, and then the more that you need to watch for your next move.

A casual observer to the market-watch shows can tell you that the talk-ing heads are wrong as often as they are right. This does not stop the "in-vesting gurus" from trotting out on the air. In a very convincing and logical way, they set the case for a certain investment or market timing activity. Interestingly, the show producers will often bring on another equally im-pressive expert to say the exact opposite and put them together on a panel. They both make a logical case; they use big, sophisticated words and have impressive credentials. Whom do we believe? Neither, because there is sim-ply no way either can know what will happen tomorrow. Any attempt to predict the future movements of the market will not consistently pay off. On these shows, pure guessing and speculating about the market is being passed off as factual, trustworthy predictions. This harms the average inves-tor more than knowing nothing about the market at all.

The truth is that the market is erratic in the short term, absolutely random. There is no way to accurately and consistently predict the future moves that the market will take before information is made publicly available. Once information is available, the market and stock prices adjust very quickly. The price of a stock already reflects all knowable and predictable information, and as things change, the market changes accordingly. To make the claim that one person knows what the market will do in the future assumes that all of the market participants who have access to the same exact information collectively have it wrong and one person can instead see what the rest do not see.

The best course is to put down the *Wall Street Journal* and turn off Jim Cramer. Instead, invest in a structurally designed, globally diversified portfolio of stocks and fixed income and ignore the media hype. Know that when the market drops, and it will, that the media is taking advantage of the fear and panic viewers experience. Take comfort in the fact that you prepared for this day, keep yourself disciplined, and surround yourself with like-minded investors. Ignoring the intense barrage of prognosticators with trends, projections, and opinions will actually help investors achieve their long-term investing goals. The smart investor knows that the daily events of the market are noise and the long-term is absolutely clear.

The Short Answer:

- **The media broadcasts stories that viewers find compelling, not to give them financial peace of mind or sound investing advice.**

QUESTION 21

How Does Asset Class Based Structured Investing Compare to Passive Indexed Investing and Active Trading?

There are three basic approaches to investing that investors can employ. Most are unaware of the distinction, yet it's absolutely vital to your long-term success with investing and peace of mind to appreciate that investing philosophy dictates everything that comes after it. The first, more traditional and widely popular approach, is called active trading. The second is called passive indexed investing, and the third is asset class based structured investing. Thus if you believe in one method, you would be uncomfortable with one of the other approaches.

Active trading garners the most attention from the media and Wall Street investment firms. This approach involves the process of seeking to attempt to identify mispricing in securities on a consistent basis. What is attractive about this method is that the manager is not locked into following any specific structure or rigid track. The money manager's sole purpose is to attempt to predict the future and take advantage of disparities; therefore, anything is on the table as long as it appears to be tied to where the market is heading. Active trading often relies on forecasting techniques to pick securities, market timing, or looking to past performance as an indicator of future trends. It almost always generates higher expenses and trading costs and excess risk, because no one can forecast or predict the future and all relevant knowable information is already reflected in the market. As a result, active traders tend to just cancel each other out, although followers of this method believe that they are reducing risk and increasing expected returns. The evidence indicates that active traders fail to outperform over 85 percent of their passive counterparts for the same level of risk in any one year.[2]

	Philosophy
Traditional Active Investing	Believes that with enough good, quality information, you or your money managers can predict the future of the market; thus it seeks to capitalize on apparent securities mispricing through forecasting and predicting the future of the market
Passive Indexed Investing	Believes that in the short term, the markets are random and unpredictable and therefore seeks to capture the entire market by rigidly tracking commercial indexes, such as the S&P 500.
Asset Class Based Structured Investing	Believes that markets work efficiently and that at any given time the market reflects all knowable and predictable information; therefore, it seeks to maximize a given level of risk by investing in the dimensions of the market that have shown to deliver the highest expected return

Passively indexed portfolio management is the opposite approach. It follows the unmistakable evidence that no one can predict the future and it's better to hold a large basket of different securities and in essence own the market itself. However, simple passive indexed funds have some serious drawbacks. While index funds follow the evidence that active trading does not work, they stop there and don't look at the evidence of what does work. Instead, they simply track commercial benchmarks to define the entire strategy. The investments are rigidly tethered to the benchmarks and thereby, by definition, have less flexibility and little ability to maximize expected return for an associated risk. This method accepts lower returns and increased trading costs in favor of tracking an artificial index.

Evidenced-based structured investing takes passive indexed investing to the next level. It is built on over fifty years of academic study and mountains of empirical research. Implementation is done by firms that follow its tenants with complete confidence in its rational basis. Further, it has shown better historical results than mere passive indexing or active trading. Instead of simply mimicking a commercial benchmark, such as the S&P 500, it looks to science to engineer prudent risk adjusted portfolios. Followers of this model believe that in a liquid securities market, prices reflect all the available information. It focuses its strategy on the dimensions of higher expected returns by employing, among other things, the multifactor model, pioneered by Eugene Fama and Kenneth French, and thereby, it seeks to add value through portfolio design and implementation.

Firms such as Dimensional Fund Advisors (DFA) have over the past thirty-plus years shown that their methods increase expected returns over the best that can be accomplished with indexed funds. In one study, researchers determined that DFA beat the best that could be generated in an indexed fund at Vanguard by 2.57 percent annually.[7] Over time, this gain will compound, generating an ever-widening gap for an investor who is not invested using a structured approach.

Those who follow the evidence are drawn to the inescapable conclusion that passive indexed investing is superior to active trading and that evidenced-based structured investing is superior to passive investing It is the responsibility of the individual investor to draw his or her own conclusions as to which philosophy he or she will employ, because in the end, an investor's philosophy must match up with his or her actions. The absence of this connection will cause fear and upset to an investor.

The Short Answer:

- **Investors must match their market philosophy to their actions to be in alignment for long-term peace of mind.**

QUESTION 22

Now that I Know How a Prudent Portfolio Is Created, Why Can't I Do This All on My Own?

Investing should seem like it follows common sense and the essential components I have told you about throughout this book. You may wonder why you can't just create a successful, prudent portfolio on your own. The answer to this is that you can but you can't.

It is possible to build a relatively diverse, low cost, passive indexed portfolio with many mainstream investment firms, such as Vanguard or Fidelity. The pitch is that the do-it-yourselfer can achieve better results than many money managers. Proponents point to some very impressive historical data to back this up. I agree; a long-term investor of low cost, indexed mutual funds holding a large basket of investments globally will outperform most active traders. This allows the possibility of achieving market rates of return without the assistance of an investment advisor or manager to exist. The problem is in the execution and staying on course with your investment philosophy.

The data that shows that most investors are not actually achieving these results is even more impressive. Investors are not achieving market rates of return over time, staying the course when times are rough, or rebalancing their portfolios periodically. When left to their own devices, the average do-it-yourself investors are not investing in a globally diversified portfolio of equities and fixed income. They are not buying low and selling high, they are not keeping their trading and turnover to a minimum, and they are not staying clear of risky investments. Investors as a group are not following the simple commonsense approach.

Where is the connection between what history tells us that we can achieve and what actual investors are earning? The independent research firm DALBAR collects data on investors. Annually, they publish what the average investor's long-term returns are on his or her investments, and each year, the numbers are unimpressive. A 1999 DALBAR study, for example, found that the average investor earned returns of 7 percent over a fifteen year period, from 1984 to 1998. The market average during the same time period was 17.9 percent. This disparity is alarming. Investors are not capturing what the market is giving us. They are largely missing the opportunities sitting right in front of them.

One of the main reasons that investors are not achieving better returns is that they are not staying with their choices long enough. They are investing in one portfolio, but if investments don't work out right away, they move on to something else and chase the hot sector. This lack of consistency and turnover often wreaks havoc on the portfolio returns.

Dysfunctional investing and other bad behaviors take shape in three common ways. The first is market timing, seeking to get in at the bottom and ride the wave up. Market timing does not work. There is abundant evidence that dispels the superstition that one can time the market. The second is to look at past performance as an indicator of what will do well next year. It has been established that the market has no short-term memory. Stock prices are random and unpredictable, and therefore, the past has no bearing on what will happen in the future. The final way to get into trouble is by individual stock picking. The notion that any person knows more than the market and can therefore outwit the system has not proven to provide any basis in truth.

The remedy for this type of flawed investing behavior is to work with an advisor, who would more accurately be called an investment coach. Your coach is someone who works with you personally and is trained in the science of investing. The coach does not just dispense general advice or execute your uninformed wishes. To be clearer, the coach offers you something you cannot get from a website, TV show, magazine, or newsletter. He or she is going to educate, or coach, you on prudent investing in a personal way.

The investment coach is critical to the success of your long-term plan. This concept is one of the hardest to accept for do-it-yourself investors. Everyone wants to believe that he or she is smart enough to execute his or her financial plan well on his or her own. To be sure, you need to be intimately involved in the process, and you need to ask the hard questions and seek to learn. You need to understand the science behind prudent investing, because without this knowledge and understanding, you will drift at the first opportunity. You will move to cash when the market is at the bottom and all the talking heads, news reports, and dinner table conversation is doom and gloom.

When you are working with an investment coach who really understands and follows the evidence and the science and math behind prudent investing, your coach is going to work hard to keep you on track, as I detail in Question 6. Your coach should have your best interest in mind. Just when you are tempted to jump ship and follow the latest craze, the hot sector, or the new IPO, your coach is going to calmly show you the evidence that doing so will probably be a huge mistake. The coach helps keep you on track and is your copilot. A good coach can make all the difference in your investment future. The true role of the investment coach is to consistently and competently speak the truth to you so that you can understand how risk and return relate and realize that there is no free lunch on Wall Street and, most important, help you find investment peace of mind and make sure that you are a winner at this game that often has many losers.

The Short Answer:

- **Investors know the rules to successful investing but easily slip into dysfunctional investing behavior. An investment coach who has the investor's best interest in mind will keep the investor on the path to success.**

ENDNOTES

1. Malkiel, Burton. *A Random Walk down Wall Street.*. W. W. Norton & Company, 1996.

2. Ellis, Charles D. *Winning at the Loser's Game*. New York: McGraw-Hill, Inc., 2013.

3. Kennon, Joshua. "Stocks Vs. Bonds Vs. Gold Returns for the Past 200 Years." Web. July 26, 2011.

4. Barro, Robert J., and Sanjay P. Misra. *Gold Returns*. National Bureau of Economic Research. February 2013.

5. Bernstein, W. J. *The Four Pillars of Investing*. New York, NY: McGraw-Hill, 2010.

6. Lardner, Jim. "Americans Agree on Regulating Wall Street." *US News*, September 16, 2013.

7. Tower, Edward, and Cheng-Ying Yang. "Enhanced Versus Passive Mutual Fund Indexing: Has DFA Outperformed Vanguard by Enough to Justify Its Advisor and Transaction Fees?" *Journal of Investing* (Winter 2008).

In creating this book, all of the content and ideas came from a collaborative learning process, where the author and collaborators worked together on common issues and questions raised by actual clients and sought to explain these concerns in an accessible way. The collaborative team consisted of Dennis Duffy, Ryan Denman, Leo McGrath, Anthony and Chris Minko, Michael and Ilana Davidov, Mark Eghrari, Victoria Rowan and Allison Tyler. While the author took the lead in putting pen to paper, the collaborators were indispensable to the final product. In the end, this book represents the collective knowledge and view of the entire team.

Michael Bonfrisco is both a licensed financial advisor and estate planning attorney, as he long ago realized that estate planning and wealth management are two sides of the same coin. With this comprehensive approach he oversees two separate firms that are devoted to providing clients with the most integrated approach possible. Michael has often said that the best will or trust is useless without a prudent well diversified investment portfolio.

Mr. Bonfrisco has been recognized as a dynamic and effective public speaker. One of his unique talents is being able to explain incredibly complex topics in a way that is accessible to the general public. His presentations have been said to be thought provoking, entertaining and informative.

Dennis Duffy is the founding attorney of the Quad City law firm, Duffy Law Office. Dennis combines an extensive background in business with a wide range of legal experience to provide his clients with a uniquely practical perspective. An attorney since 1989, he now devotes his law practice primarily to estate planning and asset protection. Mr. Duffy also offers frequent educational seminars on a variety of estate planning topics to both the general public and private groups in the Quad Cities area.

As a financial coach, Dennis has been helping clients with the clarity and education needed to be a successful investor his entire career. He obtained his Series 65 licenses in 2004 and coached hundreds of clients on how to avoid the typical myths of investing by presenting educational workshops on a variety of topics. In 2015, he was the founding partner in a Registered Investment Advisory firm, Abundance Financial Coaching LLC that offers fee only planning. He helps his clients learn how to use academic and evidence based investing to avoid stock picking, market timing and forecasting based on past performance to achieve lifelong successful financial peace of mind.

Dennis's calling as a coach is to help others understand the academic concepts and application of Free Market Portfolio Theory to change their lives. We coach investors to apply the academic principles of the Efficient Market Hypothesis, Modern Portfolio Theory, and the Three Factor Model. In addition, we help clients understand that their own behavior can be the biggest challenge to successful investing. Behavior management by coaching cannot be done by computers, robots or machines alone, if one desires to achieve lifelong investing success.

Ryan Denman is a senior associate attorney at the Quad City Law Firm, Duffy Law Office. Ryan's goal is to preserve his client's wealth while giving them peace of mind and unparalleled service. Mr. Denman's practice includes, but is not limited to, wills, trusts, estate planning and probate law. His background in economics and law allows him to give his clients all of the tools necessary for them to construct their estate plan. Mr. Denman offers frequent educational workshops on a variety of estate planning topics to both the general public and private groups in the Quad Cities area.

As a financial coach, Ryan has been helping clients with the clarity and education needed to be a successful investor. He obtained his Series 65 license in 2013 and coached hundreds of clients on how to avoid the typical myths of investing by presenting educational workshops. In 2015 he was a founding partner in a Registered Investment Advisory firm, Abundance Financial Coaching, LLC that offers fee only planning. He helps clients learn how to use academic based investing to avoid stock picking, market timing and forecasting in order to achieve lifelong successful financial peace of mind.